D1037084

DISCARD

CHICAGO PUBLIC LIBRARY
TOMAN BRANCH
2708 S. PULASKI ROAD
CHICAGO IL 60623

DEMCO

Anthrax

Titles in the Diseases and Disorders series include:

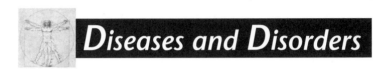
Diseases and Disorders

Anthrax

by Barbara Saffer

LUCENT BOOKS ®

THOMSON
™
GALE

San Diego • Detroit • New York • San Francisco • Cleveland
New Haven, Conn. • Waterville, Maine • London • Munich

On cover: A scanning electron micrograph of anthrax bacteria is pictured.
The blue anthrax bacterium (center) is in the process of forming spores.

© 2004 by Lucent Books. Lucent Books is an imprint of The Gale Group, Inc.,
a division of Thomson Learning, Inc.

Lucent Books® and Thomson Learning™ are trademarks used herein under license.

For more information, contact
Lucent Books
27500 Drake Rd.
Farmington Hills, MI 48331-3535
Or you can visit our Internet site at http://www.gale.com

ALL RIGHTS RESERVED.
No part of this work covered by the copyright hereon may be reproduced or used in any form or by
any means—graphic, electronic, or mechanical, including photocopying, recording, taping,
Web distribution, or information storage retrieval systems—without the written permission of the
publisher.

LIBRARY OF CONGRESS CATALOGING-IN-PUBLICATION DATA

Saffer, Barbara.
  Anthrax / by Barbara Saffer.
    v. cm. — (Diseases and disorders series)
  Includes bibliographical references and index.
  Contents: Anthrax in animals—A human scourge—Preventing and treating anthrax—
Anthrax biological weapons—Detecting and responding to anthrax bioweapons.
    ISBN 1-59018-405-X (hardback : alk. paper)
  I. Title. II. Diseases and disorders series (San Diego, Calif.)

Printed in the United States of America

R06043 01878

Table of Contents

"The Most Difficult Puzzles Ever Devised"

CHARLES BEST, ONE of the pioneers in the search for a cure for diabetes, once explained what it is about medical research that intrigued him so. "It's not just the gratification of knowing one is helping people," he confided, "although that probably is a more heroic and selfless motivation. Those feelings may enter in, but truly, what I find best is the feeling of going toe to toe with nature, of trying to solve the most difficult puzzles ever devised. The answers are there somewhere, those keys that will solve the puzzle and make the patient well. But how will those keys be found?"

Since the dawn of civilization, nothing has so puzzled people—and often frightened them, as well—as the onset of illness in a body or mind that had seemed healthy before. A seizure, the inability of a heart to pump, the sudden deterioration of muscle tone in a small child—being unable to reverse such conditions or even to understand why they occur was unspeakably frustrating to healers. Even before there were names for such conditions, even before they were understood at all, each was a reminder of how complex the human body was, and how vulnerable.

While our grappling with understanding diseases has been frustrating at times, it has also provided some of humankind's most heroic accomplishments. Alexander Fleming's accidental discovery in 1928 of a mold that could be turned into penicillin

6

has resulted in the saving of untold millions of lives. The isolation of the enzyme insulin has reversed what was once a death sentence for anyone with diabetes. There have been great strides in combating conditions for which there is not yet a cure, too. Medicines can help AIDS patients live longer, diagnostic tools such as mammography and ultrasounds can help doctors find tumors while they are treatable, and laser surgery techniques have made the most intricate, minute operations routine.

This "toe-to-toe" competition with diseases and disorders is even more remarkable when seen in a historical continuum. An astonishing amount of progress has been made in a very short time. Just two hundred years ago, the existence of germs as a cause of some diseases was unknown. In fact, it was less than 150 years ago that a British surgeon named Joseph Lister had difficulty persuading his fellow doctors that washing their hands before delivering a baby might increase the chances of a healthy delivery (especially if they had just attended to a diseased patient)!

Each book in Lucent's Diseases and Disorders series explores a disease or disorder and the knowledge that has been accumulated (or discarded) by doctors through the years. Each book also examines the tools used for pinpointing a diagnosis, as well as the various means that are used to treat or cure a disease. Finally, new ideas are presented—techniques or medicines that may be on the horizon.

Frustration and disappointment are still part of medicine, for not every disease or condition can be cured or prevented. But the limitations of knowledge are being pushed outward constantly; the "most difficult puzzles ever devised" are finding challengers every day.

A Deadly Disease

A NTHRAX IS A deadly, infectious disease caused by a bacterium, *Bacillus anthracis*. Anthrax usually attacks animals, but can also infect humans. It is one of about 150 known zoonotic diseases, which can be passed directly from animals to humans under natural conditions.

The disease now commonly known as anthrax probably originated at least eleven thousand years ago, when human beings began to domesticate animals. Over the course of history, the affliction was called by various names, including splenic fever, murrain, black bane, malignant edema, plague, and woolsorters' disease. The name "anthrax" comes from *anthrakis*, the Greek word for coal, because of the large black-crusted sores the disease often causes in humans.

Historians believe one of the first written references to anthrax is found in the Old Testament. In the book of Exodus, which describes events that occurred about 1445 B.C., God sent Moses to Egypt to persuade the pharaoh to free the Israelites. When the pharaoh refused, God inflicted a series of plagues on the Egyptians. The fifth plague was a "grievous murrain" that killed cattle, horses, asses, camels, oxen, and sheep. The sixth plague was "boils"(pus-filled blisters) that afflicted men and beasts throughout Egypt. Scholars believe both of these scourges were anthrax.

Anthrax is also mentioned in the early writings of the Egyptians, Hindus, Mesopotamians, Greeks, and Romans. In *The Iliad*, written about 800 B.C., the Greek poet Homer tells of a pestilence sent by the god Apollo to attack mules and hounds as well as people, so that "all day long the pyres of the dead were burning."[1] And in *The Georgics*, written around 30 B.C., the Roman writer Virgil describes a disease affecting farm animals that "chokes the very stalls with carrion-heaps that rot in hideous corruption [decomposition], till men learn with earth to cover them, in pits to hide." Virgil also describes how the illness spreads to people: "For e'en the fells [hides] are useless; nor the flesh [meat] with water may they purge, or tame with fire. Nor shear the fleeces even, gnawed through and through with foul disease . . . but, had one dared the loathly weeds [garments] to try, red blisters and an unclean sweat o'erran his noisome [stinking] limbs, till . . . the fiery curse his tainted frame devoured."[2]

Over the next two thousand years various parts of the world experienced human anthrax outbreaks. One of the worst occurred in 1613. A devastating pandemic, called black bane, swept across Europe, killing more than sixty thousand humans plus enormous numbers of cattle, goats, horses, and sheep. A century and a half later, in 1769, Jean Fournier classified the deadly livestock disease as anthrax or *charbon malin* (malignant black pustule).

In the early 1800s anthrax once again devastated farms in Europe. In some areas, the disease infected up to 50 percent of the sheep and 75 percent of the goats, as well as numerous people. Later, in the mid-1800s, after industrialization led to the growth of factories in western Europe, anthrax epidemics broke out among those workers who processed hair, hides, and wool. Finally, in the

This medieval illustration depicts the plague on Egyptian cattle (bottom left) described in the book of Exodus. Scientists today believe that the biblical plague was actually anthrax.

late 1800s advances in medicine helped to curtail the destruction caused by this frightful disease.

Afterward, in the early 1900s, various nations began to investigate the use of anthrax as a biological weapon. Biological weapons, designed to destroy humans, animals, or plants, are composed of microorganisms or toxins (poisons) produced by living organisms. Anthrax seemed an ideal choice for a biological weapon because *Bacillus anthracis* forms spores—dormant structures that are deadly, simple to produce, easy to store, readily spread, difficult to destroy, and hard to detect.

Small numbers of anthrax weapons were used by Germany during World War I and by Japan during World War II. Many nations continued to research anthrax weapons after World War II in an attempt to produce more deadly biological arms. Finally, an international treaty banning biological weapons went into effect in 1975, and anthrax largely receded from public awareness.

Then, in fall 2001, an unknown terrorist sent at least four letters containing lethal anthrax spores to a number of public facilities, including television and newspaper offices in New York City, media outlets in Florida, and Senate offices in Washington, D.C. The spores in the anthrax letters infected twenty-two people. Five victims died, and thousands of people were treated with antibiotics to protect them from the disease. The cleanup of contaminated facilities took from months to years, and cost hundreds of millions of dollars.

The anthrax attacks heightened public interest in this ancient disease, which, though it has become rare in industrialized nations, continues to afflict people and animals in developing countries and presents a continuing threat as a potential bioweapon.

Chapter 1

Anthrax in Animals

A LMOST ALL WARM-BLOODED animals are vulnerable to anthrax. Most anthrax victims, however, are herbivores, especially grazing animals such as cattle and sheep. Other domesticated creatures—such as horses, mules, goats, camels, oxen, and llamas—are also very susceptible to the disease. So are many wild animals. For example, anthrax is common in antelope, deer, elk, reindeer, guinea pigs, mice, and rabbits. Anthrax outbreaks caused by contaminated forage have even been reported among elephants and hippopotamuses.

Cats, dogs, pigs, and birds rarely catch anthrax, and cold-blooded creatures never do. Scientists believe that basic differences in anatomy and physiology make some animals more susceptible to certain microbes than others. Thus, many carnivores—including dogs and cats—appear to have some natural resistance to anthrax, as do some omnivores such as pigs.

For other creatures, high or low body temperatures contribute to their immunity to anthrax. *Bacillus anthracis* bacteria grow best at temperatures ranging from about 77°F to 104°F. Thus, most birds are immune to anthrax because their body temperatures average about 107.6°F. This is several degrees higher than the average body temperatures of cows, goats, and other herbivores (102.2°F) that usually contract anthrax. Conversely, the low body temperature of cold-blooded animals, which varies with the environment, helps protect them from anthrax.

In the past anthrax was common all over the world. Now, it occurs mainly in developing regions that lack the means to control the disease, such as sections of the Middle East, Africa, Australia, southern and eastern Europe, South America, Central America, the Caribbean, and Asia. In the mid-1900s, for instance, a devastating anthrax epidemic killed about 1 million sheep in Iran.

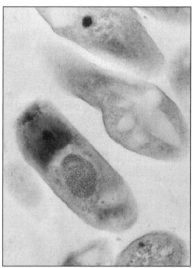

Anthrax spores (left) lie dormant until they come in contact with a warm-blooded animal. They then become active as rod-shaped bacteria (right).

In 2000 at least forty-eight countries suffered from outbreaks of animal anthrax. Of those, forty-three were developing nations, including Nicaragua, Romania, Mongolia, Tajikistan, Kazakhstan, Afghanistan, India, Ethiopia, and Zimbabwe. In January 2000 a terrible anthrax epidemic was reported on an ostrich farm in West Java, Indonesia. Unlike most birds, the average body temperature of ostriches is about 102.6°F, making them susceptible to anthrax. To eliminate the disease from the ostrich farm, over twenty-six hundred ostriches were killed with injections of strychnine (a type of poison). The carcasses were then placed in a deep pit and burned.

A number of industrialized countries, such as Canada, France, Germany, and the United States, also experienced outbreaks of animal anthrax in 2000. Anthrax is not common in the United States, but outbreaks periodically occur, especially in parts of the Southwest, Great Plains, Midwest, and Southeast. In summer 2000, for example, about sixteen hundred animals—including horses, cattle, elk, water buffalo, a llama, and twelve hundred wild, white-tailed deer—died from anthrax in Texas. In the fall of that same year, more than fifty cows died of anthrax at a ranch in Washoe County, Nevada. According to David Thain, Nevada Department of Agriculture state veterinarian, the Nevada outbreak was "believed to be due to . . . ditch cleaning that released soil borne [anthrax] spores onto pasture grasses."[3]

In 2001 approximately 100 animals in northwestern Minnesota died from anthrax, as did 21 cattle on a ranch in Santa Clara County, California. In addition, 160 animals in North Dakota perished from the disease. The outbreak in North Dakota was partly triggered by the weather, according to Larry Schuler, the North Dakota state veterinarian. "The [anthrax] spores are always in the ground," observes Schuler. "What appears to bring [anthrax] on is when we have a very wet spring with some flooding followed by a lot of hot dry weather. The spores float up to the surface in the flooding, then land on plants that the cattle eat later."[4] A similar weather pattern, hurricane rains followed by hot weather, caused anthrax to break out near Del Rio, Texas, in August 2003.

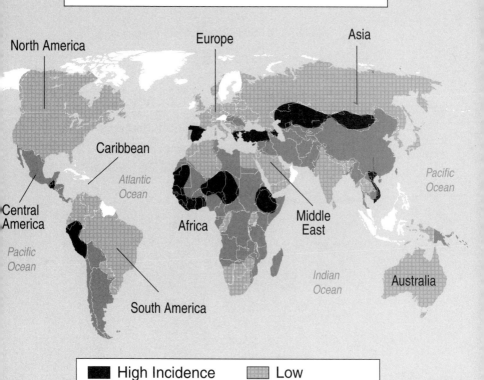

Frequency of Anthrax Cases Worldwide

North America • Europe • Asia • Caribbean • Central America • Africa • Middle East • South America • Australia • Atlantic Ocean • Pacific Ocean • Indian Ocean • Pacific Ocean

■ High Incidence   ▦ Low
■ Moderate   ☐ Probably Free

Life Cycle of *Bacillus anthracis*

Bacillus anthracis, the organism that causes anthrax, is a large, rod-shaped bacterium. Under normal conditions *Bacillus anthracis* organisms are surrounded by a gel-like covering called a capsule. This coating protects *Bacillus anthracis* organisms from the immune system of a host animal.

Anthrax organisms range in size from about 1 to 1.5 microns in width and about 3 to 10 microns in length (1 micron = 1 millionth of a meter). When exposed to adverse conditions, such as the death and decomposition of a host animal, anthrax bacteria form spores.

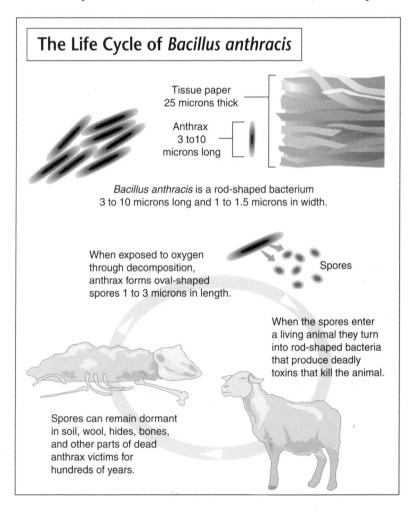

The Life Cycle of *Bacillus anthracis*

Tissue paper
25 microns thick

Anthrax
3 to10
microns long

Bacillus anthracis is a rod-shaped bacterium
3 to 10 microns long and 1 to 1.5 microns in width.

When exposed to oxygen
through decomposition,
anthrax forms oval-shaped
spores 1 to 3 microns in length.

Spores

When the spores enter
a living animal they turn
into rod-shaped bacteria
that produce deadly
toxins that kill the animal.

Spores can remain dormant
in soil, wool, hides, bones,
and other parts of dead
anthrax victims for
hundreds of years.

Bacillus anthracis organisms must be exposed to oxygen to make spores, so spore production does not occur inside intact corpses. Anthrax spores are hardy, thick-walled, oval bodies with an average diameter of about 1 to 3 microns. The spores are highly resistant to drought, heat, cold, disinfectants, and other unfavorable surroundings. The spores can lie dormant in natural environments such as vegetation, soil, or water for hundreds of years. For example, the soil of the Ohio Valley of the eastern United States—which was contaminated by the livestock of homesteaders in the early 1800s—still contains anthrax spores. The same is true of old cattle trails that ran from Texas to Canada, and routes used by pioneers in the Old West. According to Susan Jones, a veterinarian and medical historian at the University of Colorado: "The practice [in the Old West] was to let the animals die and leave them behind. The animal becomes an incubator, and the bacteria survive in spore form for decades and decades in soil."[5] Wool, hides, bones, and other parts of deceased anthrax victims can also harbor the spores for years. Lingering spores make it almost impossible to eliminate anthrax from areas where animals have been infected throughout history.

Once anthrax spores enter the body of a living animal, they germinate, or transform back into rod-shaped bacteria. The bacteria begin to multiply near the site of invasion, then spread through the creature's body and continue to reproduce. A huge population of germs develops and produces toxins, resulting in the host animal's death. As the creature's carcass breaks down, the anthrax bacteria form spores, which disperse into the surrounding environment. When the spores are consumed by an animal, the cycle begins again.

Methods of Infection

Though anthrax can strike at any time, grazing animals usually get sick in the dry summer months, when available forage decreases. The animals will eat grass to the ground and may pull plants up and eat the roots as well, taking in anthrax spores in or on the soil. The coarse vegetation can cause small cuts and abrasions in the mouth, throat, and intestine of a grazing animal, allowing the spores to enter the body. Anthrax can also be contracted by livestock through wounds caused by dehorning or castration.

Meat-eating creatures, like predators and scavengers, may contract anthrax from consuming sick prey or infected carcasses. Anthrax spores can also be transmitted by insect bites, polluted water, commercial feed made from diseased animal carcasses, and dust blown off anthrax-contaminated soil.

Once infection occurs, the incubation period, or length of time until symptoms appear, ranges from one to fourteen days but is usually from three to seven days. The course of the illness varies with the form of the disease and the animal infected.

Forms of Animal Anthrax

Four forms of anthrax are seen in animals—peracute anthrax, acute anthrax, subacute anthrax, and chronic anthrax. They differ chiefly in the span of time between the appearance of symptoms and death. Peracute anthrax generally lasts from one to two hours, though some animals go from apparent health to death in moments. Acute anthrax persists for one to two days. Subacute anthrax lasts for three to five days. Chronic anthrax persists longer than five days. Some animals recover from the chronic form of the disease.

Death from anthrax is generally due to septicemia, or blood poisoning, caused by high levels of *Bacillus anthracis* organisms and the toxins they secrete. At the time of death, most susceptible species—if left untreated—contain about 10 million to 100 million *Bacillus anthracis* organisms per milliliter (.03 fluid ounces) of blood. Large amounts of anthrax toxins result in kidney failure, tissue damage, massive edema (swelling due to accumulation of fluids in tissue spaces), and shock (decline of body functions due to reduced blood circulation). Animals that survive anthrax become immune to the disease and cannot be reinfected.

Peracute and Acute Anthrax

Ruminants, or grazing animals that chew their cud—such as cattle, sheep, goats, oxen, and llamas—usually exhibit peracute or acute anthrax, the most severe forms of the disease. Horses, which also forage in pastures, generally demonstrate peracute or acute anthrax as well.

Cattle, as well as sheep, goats, llamas, and other grazing animals, are susceptible to peracute and acute anthrax, the most severe forms of the disease.

Animals with peracute anthrax may die suddenly, without exhibiting any signs of illness. "Even if you're watching your animals like a hawk, all you might notice is a little lethargy," observes Konrad Eugster, executive director of the Texas Veterinary Medical Diagnostic Laboratory in College Station. "For all practical purposes, it's a sudden, unexplained death."[6]

Usually, though, victims of peracute anthrax exhibit a variety of symptoms such as fever, muscle tremors, difficulty breathing, and convulsions for one to two hours before death. Creatures with acute anthrax demonstrate similar symptoms for one to two days. Acute anthrax sufferers may also display chills, loss of appetite, staggering, diarrhea, convulsions, and aggressiveness (a tendency to charge) followed by listlessness. Affected animals also develop swellings, called tumors, on the body. Pregnant animals may lose the fetus, milk production may be reduced, and milk may be discolored—blood-stained or yellow. Infected horses often experience severe colic (intestinal distress).

After death from peracute or acute anthrax, there may be bloody discharges from the victim's nose, mouth, and anus; rapid bloating and decomposition of the carcass; dark, unclotted blood in the body; reduced rigor mortis (stiffening of the corpse); and an enlarged, pulpy spleen the color of blackberries. Tumors, if cut open, appear black and are filled with a bloody mass of decayed tissue.

Subacute and Chronic Anthrax

Pigs, cats, and dogs generally demonstrate subacute or chronic forms of anthrax. On rare occasions, cattle and horses also exhibit these varieties of the disease. Symptoms of subacute and chronic anthrax might include blood-stained, foamy discharges from the mouth, enteritis (inflammation of the intestine), labored breathing, difficulty swallowing, and swelling of the tongue and throat. In some cases the victim's shoulders, sides, and genital region swell also.

If the swollen throat inhibits breathing, a victim of subacute anthrax can die of suffocation. As in other types of anthrax, subacute and chronic forms of the disease often result in death from septicemia. Sometimes, though, pigs, cats, and dogs—which are somewhat resistant to anthrax—recover from the chronic form of the disease.

Cutaneous Infection

On occasion, animals become infected with anthrax cutaneously (through the skin) because of insect bites or injury. In these cases the disease remains restricted to the site of injury in the early stages. The affected area initially becomes hot and swollen, then grows cool and numb.

Without treatment the illness may become systemic seven to ten days after infection, resulting in septicemia. Death then follows within twenty-four to thirty-six hours.

Diagnosing Anthrax in Animals

If an animal perishes after exhibiting some of the symptoms described above, or dies very suddenly, anthrax is usually suspected. In such a case, veterinarians are warned not to perform a necropsy, or animal autopsy, to learn the cause of death. *Bacillus anthracis* quickly sporulates (forms spores) when exposed to air. Thus, opening the body would induce sporulation and allow anthrax to spread, endangering other animals and humans.

Instead of examining the interior of a suspected anthrax corpse, veterinarians are advised to withdraw blood from an outer vein, such as the jugular vein in the neck. Laboratory workers then prepare a slide of the blood and dye it with a bacterial Gram's stain. To perform a Gram's stain, a laboratory technician immerses the slide in the following series of solutions for about ten seconds each: a purple dye called gentian violet, iodine, alcohol, and a pink dye called safranin. When the stained slide is examined with a microscope, the presence of *Bacillus anthracis* organisms—which appear as violet blue rods containing colorless, oval spores—would demonstrate infection with anthrax.

Veterinarians must take extra care to prevent the spread of anthrax when examining the bodies of animals suspected of dying from the disease.

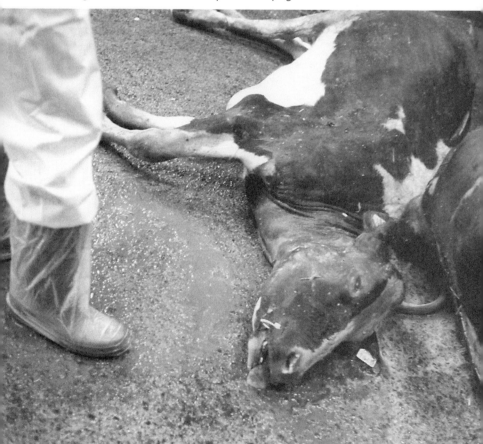

How Anthrax Spreads

Anthrax spores, which are easily dispersed, can spread the disease over an extensive area. Animal disseminators of anthrax spores include scavengers such as ravens, vultures, and hyenas that eat the carcasses of anthrax victims. Afterward, the scavengers roam around their ranges dispersing the spores in their feces. Anthrax victims may also contaminate the ground when they die, or pollute water holes if they perish there. Anthrax spores can also be spread by mosquitoes, biting flies, and other blood-sucking insects, which transmit bacteria from one animal to another.

Floodwaters can sweep anthrax spores great distances from their point of origin. Similarly, spores can be dispersed by effluents from factories that use animal parts, such as tanneries, rendering works, carpet mills, and brush factories. The waste products discharged into streams can be carried many miles. The most widespread dis-

The world's rural poor, like these Afghan shepherds, rely on livestock for their livelihood. Outbreaks of the disease decimate livestock populations, resulting in economic ruin.

persion of anthrax spores may be via commercial products made with animal parts, which are exported around the globe. These include feedstuffs, protein concentrates, raw bone meal, blood meal, and animal hides.

Economic Impact of Animal Anthrax

Outbreaks of animal anthrax can have severe economic consequences. This is especially true in developing nations, which contain large numbers of poor shepherds and farmers. At the end of the twentieth century, for example, livestock helped support at least 70 percent of the world's rural poor, estimated to be between 800 million and 1 billion people. Thus, anthrax—which can wipe out livestock very quickly—is ranked as one of the twenty conditions that have the greatest impact on poor people around the world.

Anthrax continues to be a major problem in disadvantaged communities because many indigent people lack the means to control the disease. In 2001, for example, a joint mission of the World Food Program and the United Nations Food and Agriculture Organization (FAO) found that shepherds in Afghanistan could not afford anthrax vaccines that cost less than one U.S. penny per dose. Moreover, poor farmers have small herds, so each animal is used for several purposes, such as transportation, plowing, pulling, carrying loads, and producing fertilizer (manure). In addition, livestock supply clothing (hides) and food. In fact, more than 75 percent of the food in shepherding communities comes from milk and livestock products. Thus, to a poor shepherd or farmer, the death of an animal from anthrax is a huge loss.

In some communities, moreover, livestock has enormous cultural and religious significance. The Dinka of Sudan, for instance, use cattle for marriage dowries and religious sacrifices, as well as other customs. The Dinka drink cow's milk and make it into butter and ghee, an oil for cooking. They use cattle urine for washing, dying their hair, and tanning animal hides. The Dinka employ cow dung as fuel for fires and use the resulting ashes to keep their cattle clean and to protect the animals from ticks. The Dinka also use the ashes to decorate themselves (body art) and to make a paste for cleaning their teeth. If cattle die from natural

For the Dinka of the Sudan, cattle carry tremendous religious, cultural, and economic importance. As a result, the socioeconomic impact of an anthrax outbreak is devastating.

causes or are sacrificed, the animals are butchered. The Dinka then eat the meat and tan the skins. The hides are used to make mats, drums, belts, ropes, and halters. The Dinka also use the horns and bones of the cattle to make tools and decorative items.

To the Dinka, in fact, cattle are the highest form of wealth. According to a 2002 FAO report about the socioeconomic impact of livestock diseases such as anthrax: "[In Dinka society] cattle play an essential role . . . providing not only milk and dowry but performing important social functions and determining a man's position and influence in the community. . . . Cattle provide the means by which kinship ties are made and maintained, a process for ensuring the long term viability of the household and a means of receiving support . . . in the event of disaster."[7] Thus, like other livestock keepers, the Dinka are greatly concerned about controlling anthrax. The Dinka have several names for this disease, including "jong nyal," which means a mysterious illness that comes from the sky or from God; "jong de tak," which means spleen disease, and "anguin," which means sudden death.

A February 2003 report from the Climate Information Project of the National Oceanic and Atmospheric Administration (NOAA), which monitors the impact of climate around the world, noted that anthrax had broken out in parts of Sudan during the dry season. According to the NOAA report, there were concerns that the disease would spread quickly, adversely affecting regions that were already experiencing food shortages. To deal with such outbreaks, the Dinka use not only conventional control measures such as vaccine and medicine, but also the services of a "spearmaster," who uses magic to try and ward off the disease.

A study, carried out by the International Livestock Research Institute under the sponsorship of the Department for International Development and published in 2003, notes that "finding [solutions] to the hazards that livestock are exposed to in the developing nations of the world is an excellent approach to rapidly emancipating the resource poor from starvation and poverty."[8] Hence, the Animal Production and Health Division of the FAO is fostering and encouraging programs to reduce the incidence of anthrax and other animal diseases around the world. The South African government, for example, disperses about one hundred thousand brochures annually—illustrated with drawings of sad cows—directing farmers to vaccinate their cattle. The goal of these international programs is to reduce poverty and bolster the livelihoods of disadvantaged shepherds and farmers. In addition, controlling zoonotic diseases like anthrax will improve the health of humans.

Chapter 2

A Human Scourge

A NIMALS ARE THE usual victims of anthrax, but the disease has also plagued humans since ancient times. Human anthrax is not common, but medical experts estimate that between twenty and one hundred thousand cases occur globally each year. People of any age may be infected, usually by handling contaminated hides or eating infected meat. Most human victims are those people who work with animals or animal products, such as farmers, ranchers, veterinarians, wildlife workers, butchers, and woolworkers. However, skin, wool, furs, ivory tusks, and other animal parts can harbor anthrax spores for years, spreading the disease to the general public. Unlike contagious diseases, anthrax is not spread from person to person.

Human anthrax is most common in regions where animal anthrax is widespread, such as parts of Africa, Asia, southern and eastern Europe, South America, Central America, the Caribbean, Australia, and the Middle East. In these areas, afflicted animals sometimes transmit the disease to humans. In Tajikistan in Central Asia, for example, 338 cases of human anthrax were reported in 2000. Kenya, Zambia, India, Pakistan, and Indonesia also reported significant outbreaks of human anthrax in 2000 and 2001.

Human anthrax is rare in industrialized countries like the United States. During the early 1900s about two hundred people per year contracted anthrax in the United States. By the mid-1900s, however, industrial upgrades, improved animal rearing practices, strict controls on imported animal products, and sterilization of animal skins, hides, and hair greatly reduced the incidence of human anthrax. Thus, few cases were reported in the United States by the last quarter of the twentieth century. An additional reason for the reduced incidence of human anthrax in the nation may be that most farmers and ranchers have learned to recognize anthrax in animals and avoid handling diseased creatures. "It's usually fairly obvious when you know what to look for," observes Martin Hugh-Jones, a veterinarian at Louisiana State University who monitors anthrax. "[Animal victims of anthrax] bloat up fairly quickly. . . . You get blood coming out of the nose and anus in some cases and they don't have rigor mortis."[9]

In the early stages human anthrax can resemble the bite of a brown recluse spider, a severe reaction to a smallpox vaccination, or other diseases like influenza, tularemia (a bacterial infection), or herpes simplex (a viral infection). A definite diagnosis of anthrax

Most human victims of anthrax are people who work with animals, like these cattle ranchers. Anthrax does not spread from person to person.

is made by isolating *Bacillus anthracis* organisms from a victim or by finding large quantities of "anthrax antibodies" (substances that fight anthrax germs) in a person's blood. If a victim contracts a deadly form of anthrax, an early diagnosis is important for rapid treatment and recovery.

The Disease in Humans

Three forms of anthrax are seen in human beings—cutaneous anthrax, inhalation anthrax, and intestinal anthrax. Each is contracted in a different way. Cutaneous anthrax is caught when anthrax spores enter through cuts or abrasions in a person's skin. Inhalation anthrax is contracted by breathing in anthrax spores. And intestinal anthrax results when humans ingest anthrax spores.

Cutaneous Anthrax

Cutaneous anthrax is the most common, and least deadly, form of the disease in people. Even without treatment, the majority of victims recover. At one time, medical experts believed that more than 95 percent of human anthrax cases were cutaneous. However, recent studies have shown that other types of human anthrax are more common than was previously believed.

The incubation period for cutaneous anthrax—from the time spores enter the skin until symptoms appear—ranges from twelve hours to twelve days, but is usually two to five days. During this time, the anthrax spores germinate into bacterial cells, which multiply and produce toxins. The toxins cause small red lesions, which may be either macules (flat spots) or papules (elevated spots), to erupt at the sites of infection. The red spots, which may be mistaken for pimples or insect bites, generally appear on exposed areas of the body, such as the head, neck, face, arms, and hands.

Over the next seven to ten days the red lesions grow into ulcers, called eschars, that vary from about one-half inch to two inches in diameter. The centers of the eschars become hard, black crusts, which give the disease its name. Historically, the eschars were called malignant pustules, carbuncles, or charbons. The eschars themselves usually do not hurt. However, the areas around the eschars swell as they become engorged with bacteria-filled fluids, and this

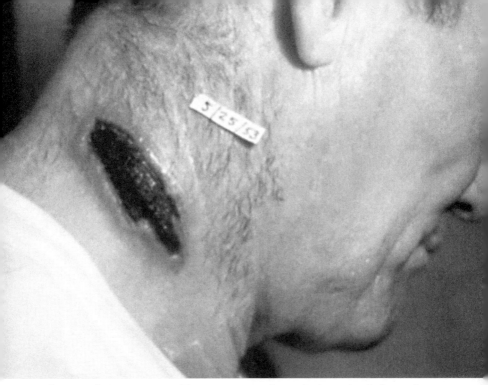

This nasty lesion was caused by cutaneous anthrax, the least deadly form of the disease. The lesions heal after one or two weeks.

may be painful. In addition, lymph nodes near the eschars, which enlarge as they help fight the infection, may also cause great discomfort.

Even without medication, 80 percent of cutaneous anthrax victims recover as their immune systems fight off the disease. In survivors, the eschars remain limited to the sites of infection and dry up and heal after one to two weeks. Permanent scars, however, may remain at the locations of the original lesions. Proper early treatment of cutaneous anthrax does not stop the formation of eschars but usually prevents death.

About 20 percent of untreated cases of cutaneous anthrax become systemic (spread throughout the body). In these cases the victims exhibit high fever, weakness, and widespread edema. Systemic cutaneous anthrax usually results in death from septicemia, caused by large quantities of *Bacillus anthracis* organisms and their toxins circulating in the blood. With appropriate early antibiotic treatment, septicemia is rare.

A possible complication of all forms of human anthrax is anthrax meningitis. This occurs when anthrax bacteria infect the membranes around the brain and spinal cord, which can result in high fever, stiff neck, severe headache, fatigue, nausea, vomiting, agitation, seizures, delirium, and coma. Anthrax meningitis almost always results in death.

Cutaneous Anthrax Outbreaks

Early in the twentieth century, several outbreaks of human cutaneous anthrax were attributed to contaminated shaving brushes. During World War I (1914–1918) large numbers of British and U.S. soldiers—as well as many British civilians—contracted cutaneous

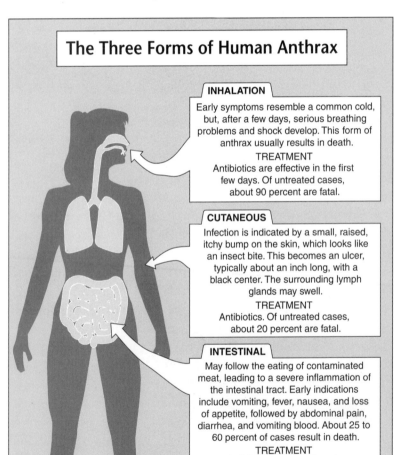

The Three Forms of Human Anthrax

INHALATION
Early symptoms resemble a common cold, but, after a few days, serious breathing problems and shock develop. This form of anthrax usually results in death.
TREATMENT
Antibiotics are effective in the first few days. Of untreated cases, about 90 percent are fatal.

CUTANEOUS
Infection is indicated by a small, raised, itchy bump on the skin, which looks like an insect bite. This becomes an ulcer, typically about an inch long, with a black center. The surrounding lymph glands may swell.
TREATMENT
Antibiotics. Of untreated cases, about 20 percent are fatal.

INTESTINAL
May follow the eating of contaminated meat, leading to a severe inflammation of the intestinal tract. Early indications include vomiting, fever, nausea, and loss of appetite, followed by abdominal pain, diarrhea, and vomiting blood. About 25 to 60 percent of cases result in death.
TREATMENT
Antibiotics like ciprofloxacin and penicillin.

Source: CNN website (www.cnn.com).

anthrax from horsehair shaving brushes purchased from Japan. The horsehair in the brushes was traced to China and Siberia. During the epidemic 149 U.S. troops stationed in Great Britain contracted anthrax, and 22 died from the disease. In the 1920s and 1930s infected shaving brushes from Japan were also responsible for cutaneous anthrax outbreaks in New York City and other parts of the United States.

Later in the century human cutaneous anthrax declined in the United States, with fewer than 230 cases reported from the 1940s through the 1990s. A number of these illnesses occurred in the 1950s, when large numbers of wool products were manufactured in the nation. During that time cutaneous anthrax outbreaks affected workers in wool and hair industries in several states, including Colorado, Pennsylvania, North Carolina, Louisiana, and New Hampshire. In 1955, for example, five workers at a mill in Monroe, North Carolina, contracted cutaneous anthrax from imported goat hair. The origin of the disease was eventually traced to a shipment of wool from Iran and Iraq. Later, in the 1970s, other cases of cutaneous anthrax occurred when infected goatskin drumheads were imported as souvenirs. In a more unusual case, a girl in Louisiana developed cutaneous anthrax after carving figures from contaminated horse bones.

Though human cutaneous anthrax in the United States is now rare, the disease is still occasionally seen in people that work with animals. In 2000, for example, a man in North Dakota developed cutaneous anthrax after disposing of five infected cow carcasses. And, in summer 2001, a ranch hand in west Texas contracted cutaneous anthrax after skinning a buffalo that had died of the disease.

Naturally occurring human anthrax is now uncommon in industrialized nations, but the disease remains a problem in developing regions. In October 2000, for instance, thirty-three people in Kazakhstan contracted cutaneous anthrax after slaughtering infected animals. Similarly, in October and November 2001, forty people in Zimbabwe developed cutaneous anthrax—also after handling meat from infected cattle. In addition, a group of San bushmen in South Africa became infected with cutaneous anthrax after butchering and cooking a dead cow found in a field.

Medical experts note that many of these human victims were among the world's poorest people, who either do not know about the hazards of anthrax or are too hungry to care. In fact, some impoverished people knowingly consume anthrax-contaminated animals rather than starve. This happened in a village of "untouchables" (the lowest caste of people) in India. Huseyin Caksen, a physician at Turkey's Yuzuncuyil University, observes: "Human anthrax will be difficult to overcome. As long as there is poverty, we will have this disease." [10]

Turkey periodically experiences human anthrax epidemics. This is especially true in rural parts of the country, where people keep livestock. In 2000, for example, 396 people in Turkey developed cutaneous or other forms of anthrax. In one instance, two children contracted cutaneous anthrax after their foreheads were smeared with infected cow's blood as part of a traditional ritual. According to researchers, blood-smearing ceremonies such as this may be a significant factor in infecting children with cutaneous anthrax in some countries.

Inhalation Anthrax

In the past, human inhalation anthrax was sometimes called "wool-sorters' disease" because of its prevalence among woolworkers in industrial mills. This form of human anthrax is uncommon, but very deadly. Without treatment, almost all victims die. With immediate, intense medical treatment, however, some patients survive.

In the United States only eighteen cases of inhalation anthrax were reported between 1900 and 1978, mostly among people who worked with goat wool or goat skins. After 1978 there were no known cases of inhalation anthrax in the United States until the anthrax mail attacks of 2001.

Inhalation anthrax is contracted when anthrax spores enter a person's lungs. The victim's immune system attacks the spores, but some spores survive and make their way to lymph nodes near the respiratory system. The spores germinate in the lymph nodes, where anthrax bacteria multiply and produce toxins. Symptoms appear soon afterwards.

In the early twentieth century, woolworkers like these were susceptible to inhalation anthrax, a form of the disease contracted when anthrax spores enter the lungs.

The incubation period for inhalation anthrax ranges from one to sixty days, but is usually between one and ten days. The first stage of the disease resembles influenza, with symptoms such as low-grade fever, chills, muscle aches, fatigue, sore throat, coughing, and headache. This phase, which can last from a few hours to a few days, is sometimes followed by a very brief period of improvement.

As the bacterial population increases and the level of toxins rises, inhalation anthrax enters the second, or fulminant (severe), stage. This phase is characterized by tissue destruction, bleeding, fluid buildup in the mediastinum (the region around the heart and between the lungs), and increased inflammation of the lymph nodes. The anthrax bacteria may also spread to the liver, spleen, kidneys, and other organs, which become dark in color and bleed.

During the fulminant stage the victim becomes extremely ill and often exhibits symptoms such as high fever, extreme shortness of breath, profuse sweating, bluish skin color, abnormally low blood pressure, vomiting, severe chest pain, abdominal pain, and shock. Up to 50 percent of people suffering from inhalation anthrax also develop anthrax meningitis. Without very early treatment, about 99 percent of inhalation anthrax victims die from septicemia two to four days after the first symptoms appear. Once the fulminant stage begins, even high doses of medicine cannot control the disease, and death follows within twenty-four hours.

A serious outbreak of inhalation anthrax occurred in 1957 at a mill in Manchester, New Hampshire. Nine laborers became ill, and four died of inhalation anthrax. Nearly a decade later, a worker at a machine shop across from the mill also died of inhalation anthrax.

Prior to 2001 the last fatal case of inhalation anthrax in the United States occurred in 1976, when a California weaver contracted the disease after working with goat hair imported from Pakistan.

Intestinal Anthrax

Human intestinal anthrax—acquired by eating meat, fruits, or vegetables contaminated with anthrax spores—has generally been considered a rare form of the disease. A report published in 2002, however, notes that intestinal anthrax is greatly underreported, especially in rural parts of developing countries. There are two reasons for this: Most doctors are not familiar with intestinal anthrax, and poor regions have too few medical clinics to adequately diagnose and report the disease.

According to Thira Sirisanthana, a professor of medicine and director of the Research Institute for Health Sciences at Chiang Mai University in Thailand, and Arthur E. Brown, chief of the Department of Retrovirology at the Armed Forces Research Institute for Medical Sciences in Thailand, human intestinal anthrax may be more common than human cutaneous anthrax in some outbreaks. The physicians observe that "in some community-based studies, cases of gastrointestinal anthrax outnumbered those of cutaneous anthrax," and "the apparently overwhelming predominance of the cutaneous form of anthrax is rather a reflection of the difficulty of diagnosis of the [intestinal] form." The scientists also assert that "mild cases of [intestinal anthrax] attract little attention, and people with severe infections, leading to death within two to three days, may never reach a medical facility."[11]

In any case, intestinal anthrax is much more serious than cutaneous anthrax. If left untreated, intestinal anthrax results in death in 25 to 65 percent of victims. In recent years known deaths from intestinal anthrax have occurred in Gambia, Uganda, Turkey, Thailand, India, and Iran. No cases of intestinal anthrax have ever been confirmed in the United States.

Eating herbivorous animals is the leading cause of intestinal anthrax in humans. The animals eat forage contaminated with anthrax spores, get sick, and die. The disease is then passed on to humans who eat their flesh. This is especially likely to occur if the meat is undercooked.

There are two types of human intestinal anthrax—oropharyngeal (mouth and throat) and abdominal—acquired when spores enter the lining of the digestive system. Oropharyngeal anthrax results when spores enter the upper digestive tract, and abdominal anthrax is contracted when spores enter the lower digestive tract. Once inside the digestive tract the spores germinate and multiply. The anthrax bacteria are then carried to nearby lymph nodes

Cases of intestinal anthrax, a form of the disease contracted through consumption of infected animals, have been documented in developing countries throughout the world.

where they continue to proliferate and produce toxins. The incubation period for intestinal anthrax ranges from one to seven days, but is usually two to five days.

Oropharyngeal Anthrax

Early symptoms of oropharyngeal anthrax may include high fever; ulcers on the mouth, tongue, tonsils, and esophagus; and inflammation of nearby lymph nodes. Swelling of the mouth and esophagus may cause trouble swallowing and difficulty breathing. If breathing problems become severe, the victim may die of suffocation. Like other forms of anthrax, untreated oropharyngeal anthrax can become systemic, leading to death from massive septicemia.

Outbreaks of oropharyngeal anthrax have been reported in Africa and Asia. In 1982, for example, in Chiang Mai, northern Thailand, the handling and ingestion of infected water buffalo meat resulted in fifty-two cases of human cutaneous anthrax and twenty-four cases of human oropharyngeal anthrax. Three of the oropharyngeal anthrax victims died. A less severe outbreak of oropharyngeal anthrax occurred in Turkey in 1986. Six people contracted the disease and three died. Seven years later, in 1993, Turkey once again experienced an outbreak of this disease.

Abdominal Anthrax

Abdominal anthrax is diagnosed more frequently than oropharyngeal anthrax. Early signs of abdominal anthrax include intestinal lesions, inflammation of abdominal lymph nodes, fever, loss of appetite, abdominal pain, vomiting, and fatigue. As the disease progresses victims experience more severe symptoms, such as fluid buildup in the abdomen, bloody diarrhea, and bloody vomit. In very severe cases the victim may die of intestinal perforation (holes in the intestine). If intestinal anthrax becomes systemic, it can resemble the final stages of inhalation anthrax and lead to death from septicemia. Death rates from intestinal anthrax are high because the disease is difficult to diagnose in the early stages. Therefore, victims may not receive timely treatment.

The worst recorded epidemic of human intestinal anthrax occurred in Saint Domingue (Haiti) in the eighteenth century and killed thousands of people. The outbreak began soon after an earth-quake demolished part of the island on June 3, 1770, destroying bakeries, homes, buildings, and food storehouses. Historian Michel-Placide Justin describes the epidemic:

> The unfortunate slaves in the north of Saint-Domingue there-fore experienced the most frightful famine. . . . The Spaniards, whose [cattle ranches] were being thinned out daily by a terri-ble [disease] . . . sought to salt or smoke all their ill or dead an-imals. . . . These meats, known as tassau in the colonies . . . spread to the slaves the [germ] of the disease. . . . A type of epidemic disease, called charbon [anthrax], spread throughout all the neighboring dwellings of the Spaniards or the routes they fre-quently used. Within six weeks, more than fifteen-thousand white and black colonists perished of this terrible disease.[12]

Another epidemic of human intestinal anthrax occurred in Udon Thani Province in Thailand in 1982. After thirty-six water buffalo and seven cattle died of anthrax, 102 people who ate meat from the infected animals became ill. Twenty-eight of those people de-veloped cutaneous anthrax, and the 74 other victims—3 of whom died—contracted intestinal anthrax.

Two years later, in 1984, an epidemic of intestinal anthrax oc-curred in Uganda when 155 people who feasted on an anthrax-infected zebu (an oxlike animal) became ill. The outbreak was reported two days after exposure, and the victims were quickly hospitalized and treated. Most of the patients recovered, but nine victims—all children—died from intestinal anthrax.

In 2000 in the United States, three people in a family of farm-ers in Minnesota developed symptoms of intestinal anthrax after eating hamburgers from a cow that had died of the disease. How-ever, the family members were treated with medication and re-covered before the disease could be confirmed.

People have sought ways to control the ravages of anthrax since ancient times. The losses caused by this dreadful disease finally began to come under control in the late nineteenth century, with the development of effective anthrax vaccines and improved treat-ments for both animals and people.

Chapter 3

Preventing and Treating Anthrax

I N THE PAST, anthrax was one of the major killers of domestic animals worldwide. Over the course of history, anthrax also caused many human deaths. The devastation wrought by this fearful affliction prompted scientists and doctors to develop methods to prevent and treat the disease.

Development and Use of Anthrax Vaccines for Animals

In 1863 the French scientist Casimir-Joseph Davaine isolated "rod-shaped organisms" from the bodies of animals that had died from anthrax. He also demonstrated that anthrax could be passed to healthy animals by injection of blood from infected creatures. In 1876 the German physician Robert Koch proved that the "rod-shaped organisms," which were *Bacillus anthracis* bacteria, caused anthrax. He also described the bacteria's life cycle. These scientific breakthroughs provided researchers with the information necessary to develop anthrax vaccines.

The first anthrax vaccine for animals contained live, but attenuated (weakened) *Bacillus anthracis* spores. The vaccine was developed in 1880 by William S. Greenfield at the Brown Animal Sanatory Institution in London. Shortly afterward, the well-known French scientist Louis Pasteur formulated a similar anthrax vaccine. Pasteur's live-spore vaccine was made from a strain of *Bacillus anthracis* that had lost some of its ability to form anthrax toxins. Thus, the anthrax bacteria in the vaccine were much less deadly than "normal" anthrax organisms.

Pasteur publicly tested his anthrax vaccine in Pouilly-le-Fort, France, in June 1881, in front of a large group of veterinarians, doctors, farmers, government officials, and reporters. After Pasteur proved that his vaccine shielded most livestock from anthrax, it was accepted for general use. Over the next fifty years the Pasteur anthrax vaccine was employed in many parts of the world to protect domestic animals from the dreaded plague. However, the Pasteur vaccine was not stable enough to be stored for long periods of time and caused serious side effects—sometimes even death—in some animals.

French scientist Louis Pasteur developed an anthrax vaccine that was used throughout the world for fifty years to protect livestock from the disease.

In 1937 the South African scientist Max Sterne developed an improved animal anthrax vaccine. Sterne's live-spore vaccine was made from a strain of *Bacillus anthracis,* called 34F, that could not form a capsule. This greatly reduced the bacteria's ability to infect animals. Sterne's vaccine, which was more stable and safer than Pasteur's vaccine, proved very effective. Hence, the Sterne vaccine—and vaccines derived from it—are used all over the world today.

For maximum protection animals must receive two injections of the Sterne vaccine, two weeks apart, followed by a yearly booster shot. Because the live-spore vaccine must germinate and grow in the vaccinated animal's body to provide protection, immunity takes from seven to fourteen days to develop. There, however, are some safety concerns associated with the Sterne vaccine. Inoculation may cause tissue damage at the site of injection, and some animals have died following inoculation.

By the late twentieth century routine vaccination had greatly reduced the incidence of animal anthrax, especially in developed countries. In the United States, for example, farmers and ranchers in spore-infected areas are advised to vaccinate, or revaccinate, their herds each year—preferably two to four weeks before "anthrax season" might be expected to begin. Konrad Eugster, executive director of the Texas Veterinary Medical Diagnostic Laboratory in College Station, advises: "If they are in an area where anthrax has been found or on a ranch that has had a case any time in the past thirty years, people should vaccinate their animals."[13] Failure to vaccinate can cause severe losses. In west Texas, for instance, anthrax outbreaks have been known to kill high-priced bulls, worth three thousand dollars or more, in minutes. Therefore, ranchers in the region usually vaccinate their livestock each spring.

Animal owners are also advised to immunize their herds after natural disasters. Following floods in Minnesota in 2002, for example, Minnesota state veterinarian Bill Hartmann recommended: "If [animal producers] are going to graze on land that flooded, they should vaccinate their animals to prevent anthrax. The way I look at it, two dollars [the price of an anthrax vaccine dose] is cheap insurance for an animal that is worth more than a thousand dollars."[14]

Ranchers vaccinate their herd against anthrax. Such precautions are taken to safeguard the ranchers' animals and protect their livelihood.

Treating and Controlling Outbreaks of Animal Anthrax

If anthrax strikes an unvaccinated herd, state veterinarians advise owners to remove livestock from the contaminated area and to treat infected animals with antibiotics (substances that kill bacteria) such as penicillin, ciprofloxacin, or oxytetracycline for at least five days. This therapy can sometimes prevent death. Farmers and ranchers are also advised to vaccinate apparently healthy animals in the herd, as well as livestock in surrounding areas. Veterinarians caution animal owners, however, not to administer vaccine and antibiotics to an animal at the same time. The antibiotics, which work by killing bacteria, will also kill the live organisms in the vaccine, rendering it ineffective. In cases of peracute anthrax, which kills within hours, effective treatment with medicine or antibiotics is not possible.

Vaccines and antibiotics are rarely used to control anthrax in wild animals. For these creatures, medicines must be administered by darting (shooting medicine-laden darts), which is difficult and expensive. However, wildlife workers in the African nation of Tanzania reportedly used antibiotics to stop an anthrax outbreak among antelopes, saving fifty animals.

If an animal dies of anthrax, medical experts recommend that the creature's carcass be deeply buried or burned without delay. Terry Conger, a veterinarian and Texas's state epidemiologist for animal disease, favors burning. "Rather than fooling with the animal carcasses, it's highly recommended that [farmers] burn that animal on site," notes Conger. "If they bury the animal, that will only preserve the [anthrax] organism deep within the soil."[15] If the carcass is buried, health authorities recommend covering it with crystalline quicklime, a powerful disinfectant. In addition, experts advise that potentially contaminated items such as food, water, bedding, blankets, fences, barns, and the soil and grass around the victim be destroyed or disinfected. Potent liquid disinfectants, approved by veterinarians, include Roccal-D, Nolvasan, and household bleach. To stop the spread of anthrax during an epidemic, farmers and ranchers are also advised to quarantine infected animals, control biting insects, and maintain good sanitation.

The World Health Organization works to educate livestock owners in Africa and other developing regions about the use of vaccine to prevent anthrax.

Promoting Anthrax Control in Developing Regions

Most countries require that anthrax outbreaks be reported to the appropriate government agencies. Veterinary officials can then supervise the medical treatment of animals, monitor the burning or burial of corpses, and take steps to prevent the spread of the disease. In poor nations, though, shepherds and farmers may not report anthrax outbreaks for several reasons: The animal owners may know little about anthrax and may not even recognize the disease in their livestock; poor farmers and shepherds consider disposing of a carcass to be a waste of meat and hides; burying the remains of anthrax victims entails extra work; and burning a carcass requires wood, which may be scarce or valuable. Thus, in poor regions animal anthrax victims are often skinned and eaten.

Livestock owners in developing nations may also resist vaccinating their herds, even if cost-free vaccine is provided by government agencies. This reluctance is caused by a variety of factors: Farmers are told to rest their animals for two weeks after vaccination, and they may not be willing to stop work for that long. Some livestock owners also believe the vaccine does not work, or fear it will actually spread the disease, because some animals—already infected with anthrax—may die in the weeks following vaccination.

To alleviate these problems, the World Health Organization (WHO) proposes that international agencies educate livestock owners in developing regions about anthrax infection and the dangers of handling, eating, or selling parts (hides, bones, meat, horns) of animals that have died from anthrax. WHO also suggests that poor animal owners be paid for correctly reporting anthrax outbreaks and for disposing of carcasses in an appropriate manner.

Development of Human Anthrax Vaccines

In 1879 John Henry Bell, a physician in Bradford, England, identified woolsorters' disease—a scourge of the wool industry—as human anthrax. Twenty-five years later Frederick Eurich, a scientist at the Bradford and District Anthrax Investigation Board, developed a method of killing anthrax spores by immersing wool and goat hair in formaldehyde, a potent disinfectant. This led to construction of the Government Wool Disinfecting Station in England in 1921, a major step toward controlling woolsorters' disease. After Eurich's death in 1945, a tribute in his hometown newspaper noted: "[Dr. Eurich was] honored wherever wool has to be handled. . . . Because of the risks he took [working with deadly spores] thousands of wool workers are alive today."[16]

Animal anthrax vaccines, not approved for people, could not be used to protect wool workers in the first half of the twentieth century. By the time Eurich died, however, human anthrax vaccines were becoming available. The former Soviet Union developed the first human anthrax vaccine, a live-spore vaccine similar to the Sterne animal vaccine, in the 1940s. Great Britain and the United States followed soon afterward, formulating human anthrax vaccines in the 1950s.

The U.S. human anthrax vaccine used today, licensed by the Food and Drug Administration (FDA) in 1970, is produced by Bio-Port Corporation in Lansing, Michigan. The vaccine, called MDPH-AVA (Michigan Department of Public Health–Anthrax Vaccine Adsorbed), is made from an unencapsulated (capsule-free) strain of *Bacillus anthracis* called V770-NP1-R, which has lost some of its ability to cause infection. The vaccine is a cell-free filtrate, containing no whole organisms. Instead, MDPH-AVA is composed of parts of *Bacillus anthracis* bacteria adsorbed (attached) to particles of aluminum hydroxide. Immunization with MDPH-AVA requires six injections: three injections given two weeks apart followed by three additional injections at six, twelve, and eighteen months. After that, yearly booster shots are needed to maintain immunity.

On the basis of a study conducted in the late 1950s, in which millworkers in four factories in New England were vaccinated, the MDPH-AVA was reported to be almost 93 percent effective. However, anthrax expert Meryl Nass disagrees. Referring to the 1950s study, she observes: "Although the study calculated vaccine effectiveness as 92.5%, I believe that all that can be said is that there is some efficacy, but the actual percent efficacy cannot be calculated due to the small number of cases [in the trial study]."[17]

The human anthrax vaccine employed in Great Britain is similar to the U.S. vaccine and about as effective. The British vaccine— a cell-free filtrate made from an unencapsulated variety of *Bacillus anthracis* called strain 34F2—is adsorbed to alum (a double sulfate of aluminum and potassium). In contrast, the human anthrax vaccines used in China and Russia are live-spore vaccines containing attenuated *Bacillus anthracis* bacteria. These vaccines—which can be injected, scratched into the skin, or administered as a spray—are thought to be very effective. In fact, according to Meryl Nass: "The efficacy of the live Russian vaccine is reported to be greater than that of the killed United States or British vaccines." [18] However, the live-spore vaccines can cause severe side effects in people, such as permanent injury to the nervous system, and are considered unsuitable for human use by many nations.

Use of Human Anthrax Vaccines

The U.S. Advisory Committee on Immunization Practices recommends anthrax vaccinations for people who may come into contact with anthrax spores, including scientists and lab workers who study *Bacillus anthracis* bacteria, employees in industries that use imported animal products, veterinarians working in anthrax-infected areas, and military personnel.

Mass vaccination of the U.S. military began in 1991 during the first Persian Gulf war with Iraq. Because government officials feared Iraq might use biological weapons containing anthrax, soldiers

A recruit is vaccinated against anthrax before her ship arrives in the Persian Gulf in 1991. Officials feared Iraq would use anthrax as a weapon during the Gulf War.

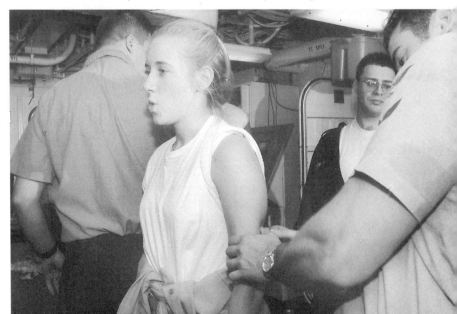

sent to the Persian Gulf received anthrax vaccinations. Six years later, in 1997, the U.S. Department of Defense (DoD) decreed that all active military personnel must be vaccinated against anthrax. The mass vaccination program began in 1998. Thus, since the early 1990s millions of American soldiers have been inoculated with MDPH-AVA.

U.S. health administrators have not recommended anthrax in-oculations for the general public for several reasons: The danger of exposure to anthrax is considered remote; the vaccination pro-cedure for MDPH-AVA is complex (six injections plus booster shots); the program would be expensive; and many people might resist being vaccinated. Even for at-risk groups, government offi-cials recommend vaccinating only healthy individuals from eigh-teen to sixty-five years of age, because anthrax vaccine studies have been restricted to that population. In addition, authorities advise against inoculating pregnant women and children, since vaccine safety has not been established for these groups.

Some experts who doubt the effectiveness and safety of MDPH-AVA have reservations about its widespread use for humans. For example, Meryl Nass observes:

> There is essentially no good data [about MDPH-AVA]. The one study of this vaccine . . . only performed active surveillance for forty-eight hours [after inoculation] and one nurse was dis-couraged from reporting [unfavorable] reactions at the site that administered the most vaccine. We do know . . . that one vacci-nated worker took his mask off in an anthrax "hot room" at Fort Detrick, got a whiff of anthrax and died.[19]

Peter C.B. Turnbull, another authority on anthrax, also questions the performance and safety of the vaccine. He notes:

> Tests in animals have indicated that the protective efficacies of both the United Kingdom and United States vaccines are less than ideal. In addition . . . the injection into human beings of crude and undefined preparations is increasingly regarded as unsatisfactory, particularly, as in the case of the anthrax vaccines, when they are associated with frequent complaints of unpleas-ant side-reactions.[20]

Adverse Reactions to Human Anthrax Vaccine

Information about adverse, or unfavorable, reactions to human vaccination in the United States is reported to the Vaccine Adverse Event Reporting System (VAERS), a joint program of the Centers for Disease Control and Prevention (CDC) and the Food and Drug Administration (FDA). Since 1990 VAERS has received over 120,000 reports from a variety of sources, including vaccine manufacturers, health care providers, state immunization programs, and vaccine recipients.

According to VAERS's records, the most common side effect of inoculation with MDPH-AVA, seen in about 30 percent of recipients, is slight tenderness and redness at the injection site. A more serious reaction, observed in about 5 percent of vaccinated people, is temporary swelling or hardening of the skin around the injection site. A small number of recipients experienced additional side effects, such as headache, itching, fever, chills, nausea, joint pain, body aches, or fatigue.

VAERS's files and physicians' records indicate that about 5 percent of inoculated people experience severe reactions to MDPH-AVA, resulting in hospitalization or permanent disability. Dangerous complications include pneumonia, seizures, inflammation of the spinal cord, heart disease, blood poisoning, infection of tissues beneath the skin, inflammation of blood vessels, loss of red blood cells, severe allergic reactions, connective tissue disease, immune system disorders, and Guillain-Barré syndrome (inflammation of the nerves, resulting in temporary loss of feeling and movement). Anthrax inoculations can also cause endocrine glands to fail (the thyroid gland, testes, and adrenal glands stop producing hormones) and Stevens Johnson syndrome (severe skin rashes in which all the skin peels off). Moreover, in a 2002 letter to *Emergency Medical News*, anthrax expert Meryl Nass writes that "Some . . . research . . . suggested that four autoimmune diseases and two cancers were statistically related to anthrax vaccination. . . . These conditions are multiple sclerosis, diabetes, asthma, Crohn's Disease [an inflammatory disease of the gastrointestinal tract], thyroid cancer and breast cancer." Nass also observes that "Currently, a number of lawsuits are in the courts related to problems

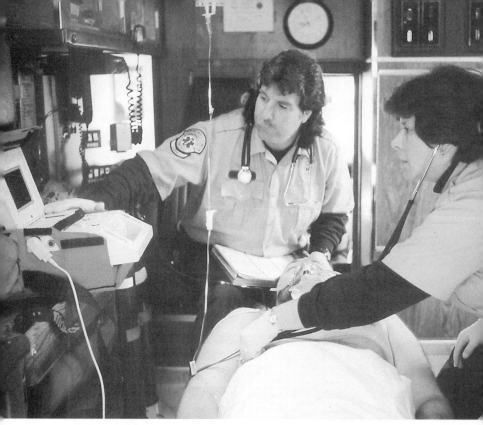

Adverse reactions to anthrax vaccine call for immediate treatment to prevent complications from setting in.

with the anthrax vaccine; several involve deaths following anthrax vaccinations."[21]

Furthermore, the number of adverse reactions to anthrax vaccine may be higher than that reported to VAERS. A 2002 report from the U.S. General Accounting Office (GAO), which monitored anthrax vaccinations among reserve members of the air force and national guard, notes that "the overall rate reported for adverse reactions was nearly three times that published in the vaccine manufacturer's product insert, which claimed only thirty percent would experience some adverse reaction." The GAO report also observes that "among those who took one or more shots . . . eighty-five percent reported experiencing some type of reaction . . . [and] of those experiencing side effects, twenty-four percent had adverse effects considered serious enough for the shots to be discontinued."[22]

Additionally, little research has been done on the long-term effects of MDPH-AVA. One published study, which monitored laboratory workers in Fort Detrick, Maryland, for twenty-five years following vaccination, concluded that they did not develop any serious ailments such as cancer or infertility from the anthrax vaccine. Because of the small number of published accounts, though, the Institute of Medicine of the National Academy of Sciences reported that it could not determine whether anthrax vaccination results in long-term health problems. To find out whether serious illnesses such as cancer are really related to anthrax vaccinations, the DoD is now doing extended studies of MDPH-AVA recipients.

Besides the concerns about side effects and serious illnesses discussed above, there is some concern that anthrax vaccination may be linked to "Gulf War syndrome," an illness experienced by some veterans of the 1991 Persian Gulf War.

Anthrax Vaccine and Gulf War Syndrome

Of the nearly seven hundred thousand U.S. troops that participated in the Persian Gulf War in 1991, over one hundred thousand became ill after returning home. The ailing soldiers reported a variety of symptoms such as headaches, skin rashes, diarrhea, fatigue, confusion, fever, night sweats, joint and muscle pains, dizziness, loss of memory, sleep disturbances, abdominal bloating, lingering bronchitis, vision problems, irritability, and depression. These symptoms are not consistent with any specific disease and were collectively named Gulf War syndrome or Gulf War illness.

The cause of Gulf War syndrome has not been determined. Health officials have suggested a number of possible causes, including side effects of medications or vaccines given to soldiers, exposure to chemical weapons, exposure to biological weapons, exposure to radiation, combat stress, or some combination of these factors.

Many government health officials do not believe the illnesses were caused by the MDPH-AVA. However, the Rockefeller Report of the Senate Committee on Veterans Affairs, issued in 1994, notes:

> Although anthrax vaccine had been considered approved prior to the Persian Gulf War, it was rarely used. Therefore, its safety, particularly when given to thousands of soldiers in conjunction with other vaccines, is not well established. Anthrax vaccine

should continue to be considered as a potential cause for undiagnosed illnesses in Persian Gulf military personnel because many of the support troops [noncombat troops] received anthrax vaccine, and because the Department of Defense believes that the incidence of undiagnosed illness in support troops may be higher than in combat troops. [23]

Experts also note that, during a conflict, soldiers are likely to receive anthrax vaccine in combination with other medications. This might have unfavorable health effects. Meryl Nass observes:

Since anthrax vaccine in the future is likely to be used in concert with other [preventive] measures against threat agents like *Clostridium botulinum* [bacteria that cause botulism] . . . safety should be demonstrated both when the vaccine is used alone, and also when it is used with other measures, including use with other vaccines and chemical protective agents, such as pyridostigmine and atropine [both used to counteract the effects of nerve gas] and so on. [24]

Though vaccination with MDPH-AVA may prevent anthrax, many people—especially civilians—have not been inoculated against the disease. If these people are exposed to anthrax, swift medical treatment may prevent serious illness or death.

Treatment for Human Anthrax

If people contract anthrax, antibiotics are used to treat them. Approved antibiotics for anthrax include ciprofloxacin, penicillin, tetracycline, doxycycline, and a number of others. To work well, the antibiotics must be administered during the disease's incubation period or within one day of the appearance of symptoms, before the bacteria begin producing deadly toxins.

Health officials also recommend that antibiotics be administered to people who have been exposed to anthrax spores but show no signs of illness. For example, physicians recommend that people who have had contact with spores, especially airborne spores that cause inhalation anthrax, be treated with "preventive" antibiotics for up to sixty days. Such at-risk individuals may also receive anthrax vaccine as a protective measure.

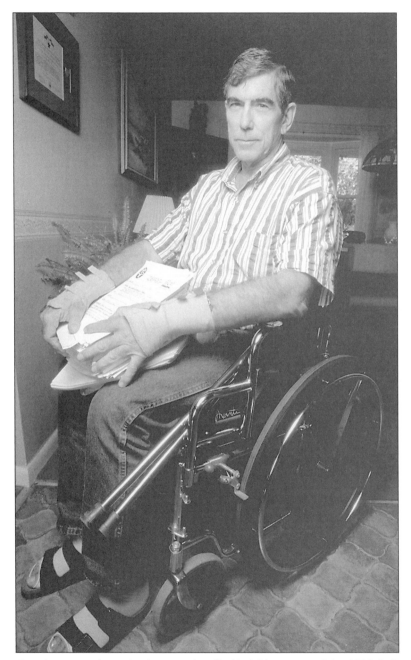

An adverse reaction to anthrax vaccine disabled this veteran of the 1991 Gulf War. Vaccine-related illnesses affected thousands of troops.

On occasion, antibiotics administered to anthrax victims cause side effects. Adverse reactions to ciprofloxacin, for example, include diarrhea, nausea, vomiting, skin rashes, headache, stomach pain, mental confusion, tremors, seizures, hallucinations, torn tendons, and allergic reactions. Doxycycline is thought to induce fewer side effects but may cause nausea, vomiting, headache, chest pain, facial swelling, throat and tongue inflammation, itching, and hives.

Development of additional antibiotics and other means of combating anthrax has become especially important in recent years because of the growing threat that rogue countries and terrorist groups will use anthrax as a biological weapon.

Chapter 4

Anthrax Biological Weapons

B IOLOGICAL WEAPONS ARE sometimes called weapons of mass destruction (WMD) because they can kill huge numbers of people with a single use. For example, a 1993 study conducted by the U.S. Congressional Office of Technology Assessment found that spraying 100 kilograms (220 pounds) of dried anthrax spores over Washington, D.C., would cause between 1 million and 3 million deaths.

Biological warfare began centuries ago, when humans first realized that illnesses could be spread by diseased people. Some of the earliest biological weapons were diseased corpses, flung into an opponent's wells or camps to sicken enemy populations. In 1346, for example, Tatars attacked Caffa, an Italian trading post in the Crimea, on the Black Sea. During the siege the Tatar army was struck by bubonic plague, which killed thousands of soldiers. The Tatars turned their dead troops into weapons, catapulting disease-ridden corpses over the walls of Caffa. According to an Italian observer, Gabriel de Mussis, "[The Tatars], fatigued by such a plague and pestiferous disease, stupefied and amazed, observing themselves dying without hope of health, ordered cadavers placed on their hurling machines and thrown into the city of Caffa, so that by means of these intolerable passengers the defenders died widely." [25] The residents of Caffa, being massacred by the plague, fled back to Italy—taking the disease with them. From Italy, bubonic plague spread across Europe, causing an epidemic of the "Black Death" that wiped out a third of the continent's population. Plague-ridden

The residents of ancient Athens despair after the city is struck with plague. Armies of the past infected the populations of enemy cities by exposing them to corpses of plague victims.

corpses were used again in 1710, when Russian soldiers employed them against Swedish troops.

Over the course of time other microorganisms have also been used as bioweapons. The British, for example, used smallpox against Native Americans in the 1760s. Over two centuries later, between 1978 and 1980, anthrax bioweapons were used to devastating effect in Rhodesia (now Zimbabwe) during that country's civil war. Records indicate that there was a huge number of animal victims as well as almost eleven thousand cases of human anthrax, with 182 human deaths. Experts believe Rhodesia's white ruling regime, in an attempt to defeat the Rhodesian natives' push for independence, spread anthrax spores over tribal lands.

By the 1900s biological weapons had become highly diverse and sophisticated. In 1925 Winston Churchill, who later became prime minister of England, wrote about "pestilences methodically prepared and deliberately launched upon man and beast. . . . Blight to destroy crops, anthrax to slay horses and cattle, plague to poison not armies only but whole districts—such are the lines along which military science is remorselessly advancing." [26]

Experts say that a catastrophic biological weapon, sometimes called "a poor man's atom bomb," can be made from readily available laboratory equipment and the anthrax spores extracted from a pailful of dirt. Thus, U.S. officials fear that rogue countries and terrorist groups might produce arsenals of these arms. When asked how seriously he took the risk of a bioterrorist attack, former director of the U.S. Central Intelligence Agency James Woolsey said, "Quite seriously. The problem is that it is comparatively easy to do compared with other acts of terrorism using weapons of mass destruction."[27]

Many biological agents, including organisms that cause smallpox, cholera, typhoid, typhus, yellow fever, and botulism, may be used as biological weapons. However, Woolsey indicates that he was especially apprehensive about terrorists using anthrax weapons because "a lot of the information about it is out there and public. . . . It's extremely lethal. It's been around a long time and a lot of people know a good deal about it."[28]

Access to Anthrax

Cultures (stocks) of deadly organisms such as anthrax are relatively easy to obtain. The American Type Culture Collection in Maryland, for instance, supplies samples of microorganisms to laboratories for medical research, vaccine production, and other lawful purposes. Moreover, there are about fifteen hundred other germ banks in the world that provide similar services. On occasion, however, germ banks have inadvertently sent microorganisms to rogue nations and terrorist groups. In the 1980s, for example, the American Type Culture Collection sold *Bacillus anthracis* bacteria to Iraq, before that country's biological weapons program became public knowledge.

Because of such mishaps, the U.S. Federal Bureau of Investigation and federal health officials invoked new rules in 1995 to control access to deadly microorganisms. The new regulations require U.S. laboratories studying lethal microbes to register with federal health administrators and be open to inspections. These rules, however, apply only to facilities based in the United States. Germ banks in other countries are governed by different rules and might still unintentionally provide virulent microbes to outlaw organizations. Moreover, criminal dealers with access to germs, or germ banks in countries with little regulation, can sell microbes to anyone. In fact, Osama bin Laden, head of the al-Qaeda terrorist organization, bought anthrax cultures from labs in Asia, according to a former follower.

Even without access to germ banks, though, anthrax spores can be obtained relatively easily from contaminated soil. James Woolsey notes: "Anthrax can be cultured from what you can get from a lot of cow pastures in the world. Making it is a little bit harder than running a micro-brewery attached to a restaurant and making beer, but it's not radically harder. . . . It is nothing like the difficulty, for example, of obtaining fissionable material and building even a primitive nuclear weapon." [29]

The First Anthrax Weapons

Research on *Bacillus anthracis* weapons began almost one hundred years ago. The first recorded use of anthrax bioweapons occurred during World War I (1914–1918). Germany sent saboteurs to a number of nations—including Argentina, Norway, Romania, Spain, and the United States—to infect sheep, cattle, horses, mules, and Norwegian reindeer with anthrax and glanders (another bacterial disease). The animals were either injected with microbes or fed sugar laced with germs. Germany's aim was to deprive the Allies of these animals, meant to be used for food and transportation. The German bioweapons did not seriously damage the Allied war effort, however, and the Allies went on to win the war.

The Geneva Conference

The use of biological and chemical weapons during World War I horrified the public and resulted in the Geneva Conference of 1925. This led to the "Geneva Protocol for the Prohibition of the Use of Asphyxiating, Poisonous or Other Gases, and of Bacteriological [biological] Methods of Warfare." The treaty allowed research into biological weapons but prohibited their use—unless someone else used them first. France, Great Britain, and the Soviet Union signed the protocol, but the United States and Japan did not. In any case,

Osama bin Laden, leader of the al-Qaeda terrorist network, is reported to have bought anthrax spores from an Asian lab to use against Western nations.

no provisions were made to enforce the treaty, and most countries ignored it. Hence, before and during World War II, in the 1930s and 1940s, many nations continued to develop biological weapons.

Japan's Biological Weapons

Japan had an extensive biowarfare research program and built a huge compound, called Manchukuo Unit 731, to manufacture biological weapons and experiment on humans. The research complex was located in Manchuria, a region of northeast China that Japan had conquered. There, Japanese scientists had access to a large supply of Chinese and Soviet prisoners of war as well as to a number of American and British detainees. Thousands of prisoners in Manchukuo Unit 731 were deliberately infected with diseases—including cholera, plague, typhoid, dysentery, and anthrax—and studied by Japanese doctors.

During war crimes trials after World War II, Major Karasawa Tomio, chief of the Japanese biological warfare unit, testified about experiments done in Manchukuo Unit 731. Tomio admitted that he

> personally was present on two occasions . . . when the action of bacteria was tested on human beings under field conditions. . . . The first time . . . toward the end of 1943 . . . some ten persons were tied to stakes . . . and a fragmentation bomb was exploded by electric current fifty meters away from them. A number of the experimentees were injured by bomb splinters and simultaneously . . . infected with anthrax.[30]

Other human subjects were secretly fed anthrax-contaminated food and liquids.

Japan's bioweapons were not confined to Manchukuo Unit 731. During World War II (1939–1945) the Japanese Imperial Army spread deadly diseases to at least eleven Chinese cities. Various means were used to distribute anthrax bacteria and other germs, including contaminating food and water supplies and dropping germ-laden feathers and cotton wadding from aircraft. Japan also used *Bacillus anthracis* bombs to spread anthrax. Shrapnel from the bombs infected people with the disease. Sheldon Harris, a historian at California State University at Northridge, estimates that more than two hundred thousand people were killed by Japan's biological weapons.

Biological Weapons Research in Great Britain

The Allies—France, Great Britain, the Soviet Union, and the United States—did not use biological weapons during World War II but did continue to research them. In the early 1940s Great Britain wanted to determine how much anthrax would be needed to attack enemy cities. Accordingly, in 1942 British scientists built a twenty-five-pound bomb, eighteen inches high and six inches wide, and filled it with anthrax spores. The bomb was exploded over a flock of sheep on

Gruinard Island, off the northwest coast of Scotland. In the days after the bomb was detonated, large numbers of sheep died of anthrax. This proved that *Bacillus anthracis* weapons could be produced and exploded without destroying the disease-causing bacteria.

In other experiments performed during 1942 and 1943, Britain exploded more anthrax bombs over Gruinard Island. After each trial, diseased sheep carcasses were hauled to the rim of a nearby cliff and tossed over. Eventually, the cliff face was blown up with explosives, blanketing the carcasses with rocks. The British tried to disinfect the remainder of the island by burning off the vegetation, but were unsuccessful. Thus, Gruinard Island was sealed off and became known as "Anthrax Island." Warning signs were posted around the rim of the island that read:

GRUINARD ISLAND
THIS ISLAND IS
GOVERNMENT PROPERTY
UNDER EXPERIMENT
THE GROUND IS CONTAMINATED
WITH ANTHRAX AND DANGEROUS
LANDING IS PROHIBITED[31]

More than forty years later, in 1986, the island was finally decontaminated with a mixture of formaldehyde and seawater and reverted to normal agricultural use.

Gruinard Island (foreground), off the coast of Scotland, was used as a testing site for anthrax bombs during World War II.

Britain also devised a method to infect cattle with anthrax, call-ing it "Operation Vegetarian." Starting in 1942, the British government made arrangements to acquire 5 million linseed oil cattle cakes (a type of cattle food), laced with anthrax, to drop on Germany in summer 1944. The goal of Operation Vegetarian was to destroy the German beef and dairy herds and to spread anthrax to the German population. The anthrax cakes were not used, however, since the Allied war against Germany was going well by 1944.

Development of Biological Weapons in the United States

During World War II the United States established a biological weapons research center in Camp Detrick, later renamed Fort Detrick, Maryland. With the assistance of Great Britain, the United States built its first *Bacillus anthracis* bomb in 1943. By May 1944 the

An American scientist works to develop an anthrax bioweapon in the 1950s. In 1969 President Nixon banned the use of biological weapons by the U.S. military.

United States had five thousand anthrax bombs, and by July 1944 the nation was capable of building fifty thousand anthrax bombs a month. U.S. military leaders wanted to be able to exterminate a huge portion of the enemy's population to stop them from fighting. However, the anthrax bombs were not used during the war.

Soon after World War II ended, the "Cold War" began. This was a long period of hostility between the United States and its allies and the Soviet Union and its confederates. Nations on both sides of the conflict continued to develop biological weapons.

In the United States, William C. Patrick III—a scientist and leading expert on biological weapons—became chief of product development at Fort Detrick. Dr. Patrick's team of researchers soon produced exceptionally deadly anthrax germs, called "weaponized" anthrax. Weaponized anthrax is composed of smooth, uniformly sized anthrax spores with no electrostatic charge, so they do not clump together. Instead, upon release the spores sail into the air, float long distances, and, when inhaled, adhere to human lungs. In addition, a single gallon of weaponized anthrax contains 8 billion lethal doses, enough to kill every person on Earth.

The U.S. military, however, needed a way to disperse the anthrax effectively; so, in 1949 the army began a series of secret outdoor experiments to find the best way to spread anthrax over Soviet cities. For the trials, the army used *Bacillus globigii*. This is a common, relatively harmless bacteria, with particle size and dispersal characteristics similar to anthrax. During the army's trials cluster bombs loaded with *Bacillus globigii* were dropped on St. Louis, Missouri; Minneapolis, Minnesota; and Winnipeg, Canada. From these tests, scientists tried to estimate the amount of anthrax needed to destroy the populations of Soviet cities like Kiev, Leningrad, and Moscow.

In another series of experiments, the U.S. Army released *Bacillus globigii* and *Serratia marcescens* (another common, rod-shaped bacteria) at various sites in the country, including New York City; San Francisco, California; Washington, D.C.; Key West, Florida; Panama City, Florida; and parts of Alaska and Hawaii. As before, the army's goal was to find the most effective means of spreading the microorganisms. The United States stopped releasing live bacteria in populated regions in 1969, when President Richard

M. Nixon banned the nation's use of offensive biological weapons. Nixon issued a memorandum declaring, "The United States shall renounce the use of lethal methods of bacteriological/biological warfare [and] . . . the United States will confine its biological research to defensive measures such as immunization and safety."[32] Nixon restricted biological weapons research to defensive purposes, noting that "mankind already carries in its own hands too many of the seeds of its own destruction."[33]

By the time the army's outdoor experiments ended, though, the tests had already exposed millions of Americans to various kinds of bacteria. When the secret trials became public knowledge during U.S. Senate hearings in 1977, army experts insisted that the bacteria were harmless. Civilian doctors disagreed, however. They observed that "harmless" bacteria such as *Bacillus globigii* can infect people weakened by other conditions such as recent surgery, deep wounds, and immune system ailments. Moreover, *Serratia marcescens* can cause serious illnesses, including blood poisoning, urinary system infection, respiratory system infection, and infection of the endocardium (lining of the heart).

The Biological Weapons Convention

Because the Geneva Protocol of 1925 failed to curb the development of biological weapons, another treaty was written almost a half-century later. The Convention on the Prohibition of the Development, Production, and Stockpiling of Bacteriological [biological] and Toxin Weapons and on Their Destruction, also known as the Biological Weapons Convention (BWC), was ready for signing in 1972. The treaty forbids development, production, stockpiling, acquiring, or keeping biological agents or toxins "that have no justification for prophylactic [preventive], protective or other peaceful purposes."[34] The BWC also requires that all biological weapons be destroyed. The treaty does allow possession of biological agents for peaceful or defensive purposes such as medical studies or vaccine production.

The BWC went into effect on March 26, 1975, and was eventually signed by 146 countries, including China, France, Great Britain, the United States, Iraq, and the Soviet Union. However, both Iraq

U.S. Marines train for biowarfare wearing protective suits. Although the use of bioweapons is prohibited by international law, the military is prepared for such an eventuality.

and the Soviet Union disregarded the treaty and continued to produce anthrax and other biological weapons. There is evidence that the United States did also. In a September 2002 article in the *Los Angeles Times*, Barbara Hatch Rosenberg, chair of the Federation of American Scientists' Biological Arms Control Program, writes:

> It was recently revealed that an Army laboratory in Utah has been secretly making weaponized anthrax for some years. Another secret project involved the construction of bomblets designed for dispersion of biological agents, although the Biological Weapons Convention explicitly prohibits [this]. . . . Such projects have raised suspicions abroad that the U.S. continues to develop biological weapons. [35]

Anthrax Research in the Soviet Union

The Soviet Union's ongoing biological weapons research was demonstrated in spring 1979, when anthrax broke out in Sverdlovsk (now Yekaterinburg), a Russian city in the Ural Mountains.

Seventy-nine residents of Sverdlovsk became ill, and at least sixty-six people died of inhalation anthrax. Numerous sheep and cattle also perished. The Soviet government quickly vaccinated thousands of residents of Sverdlovsk and instituted a massive cleanup of the city.

Soviet officials blamed the outbreak on contaminated meat, but experts in other countries attributed it to an inadvertent release of anthrax spores from the Microbiology and Virology Institute in Sverdlovsk, a suspected biological weapons facility. In 1992, after the Soviet Union broke up, Russian president Boris Yeltsin admitted that the anthrax outbreak had been caused by an accident at a biological warfare plant. A small amount of anthrax spores had escaped from the Microbiology and Virology Institute and had been blown over the city by winds.

More evidence that the former Soviet Union had violated the BWC was revealed in 1992, when Soviet bioweapons expert Ken Alibek (formerly Kanatjan Alibekov) defected to the United States. Alibek had been deputy chief of research at the world's largest biological weapons facility, located in the Soviet Union. When questioned, Alibek acknowledged "the Soviet Union had four major anthrax production facilities. . . . And I became commander of . . . the Stepnogorsk facility [in northern Kazakhstan] in 1983 . . . with the specific task to develop new anthrax biological weapons."[36] Alibek admitted that his research team produced large quantities of weapons-grade anthrax, which was loaded into bombs and missiles in 1989. Some military authorities believe these and other Soviet biological weapons may have been able to wipe out the populations of entire countries.

In 1992 Soviet bioweapons chief Ken Alibek revealed that his research team had produced large quantities of anthrax.

Alibek also revealed that, following the collapse of the Soviet Union in 1991, a number of his fellow scientists were hired by outlaw states like Afghanistan, Iran, and Iraq to help them develop bioweapons. This is especially worrisome to U.S. biological weapons experts. During an interview in 2001 William C. Patrick commented, "My biggest concern now is a rogue country that supports state terrorism and has the facilities to prepare . . . a good dry powder of anthrax . . . [and] my second biggest concern is what is happening to the scientists of the former Soviet Union who have the techniques and the knowledge base to manufacture a weapons agent." [37] Anthrax in dry powder form is more deadly than bacteria-filled liquids, which are easier to produce. According to anthrax expert Ken Alibek, anthrax powder is extremely lethal because "the dry clumps of spores that are each between one and five microns wide [are] the optimal size to penetrate a human lung and stay there." [38]

Further Proliferation of Biological Weapons

U.S. administrators believe that by the beginning of the twenty-first century, about seventeen countries had biological weapons. These included Taiwan, China, India, Pakistan, Egypt, Israel, Syria, Iran, North Korea, Russia, Libya, Sudan, Yemen, Zimbabwe, South Africa, and Iraq (before the United States and its allies invaded in 2003). Authorities fear that an unknown number of terrorist groups may also have biological weapons, since the information needed to produce these arms is available on the Internet and in books. Moreover, crude biological weapons can be made by just a few people working in a small space.

By the late 1990s the possible use of bioweapons by outlaw nations and terrorist groups was especially troubling to the United States and other Western nations.

Aum Shinrikyo Terrorists Use Anthrax Weapons

At the end of the twentieth century, Aum Shinrikyo ("Supreme Truth") was a shadowy Japanese cult that wanted to take over the world with the help of WMDs. The cult obtained *Bacillus anthracis* from a university and grew the bacteria in large drums of liquid in the basement of its eight-story headquarters near Tokyo. Then, in July 1993 Aum Shinrikyo pumped the liquid to the building's roof and sprayed it into the air for twenty-four hours. No one was injured or killed during this incident.

Later that year Aum Shinrikyo released anthrax spores around Tokyo eight more times, using van-mounted sprayers. Again, no sicknesses or deaths were reported. Since the anthrax caused no ill-nesses, Japanese authorities did not learn of the at-tacks until two years later, when cult members were tried for releasing sarin nerve gas in subways.

Japanese officials surmised that the cult's anthrax cultures must have been defective. This was proven true in 2001, when Paul Keim, anthrax specialist at Northern Arizona University, analyzed Aum Shin-rikyo's anthrax cultures. Keim's studies showed that the cult dispersed the Sterne 34F2 strain of an-thrax, which Japan uses to make animal vaccines. This unencapsulated strain does not cause disease.

Some weapons experts speculate that Aum Shinrikyo might have unknowingly used a non-virulent strain of anthrax, or that they were test-ing their equipment for a later deadly attack.

Keim has another theory. He suggests that the cult members may have been forced to unleash the attack before they were ready out of fear of their leader, Shoko Asahara, who was known to murder anyone that angered him. Keim surmises that "when Asahara or-dered in 1993 that a biological weapons attack be carried out, Aum members were probably too afraid to acknowledge that they did not have the necessary materials, so they attempted to obtain what-ever they could quickly get their hands on, leading to the failed attack."[39]

Deploying Anthrax Weapons

Because anthrax is not contagious, only people directly exposed to the spores can become infected. To be effective, therefore, anthrax

Members of the Japanese cult Aum Shinrikyo tried to infect the city of Tokyo with anthrax in 1993. The strain of anthrax the cult used, however, was not infectious.

bioweapons must release a vast number of spores. Nations, which generally have armies and military equipment, have more options for deploying anthrax weapons than do terrorist groups. Leroy D. Fothergill, former director of the biological weapons laboratories at Fort Detrick, observes that there are two ways of launching an attack with bioweapons: "The first, and most important of these, is through overt military delivery through weapons systems designed to create an aerosol or cloud of the agent. The second would be through covert [undercover] methods."[40]

Military options for spreading anthrax bioweapons include artillery, rockets, and aerosol bombs. Other options include manned aircraft such as piloted fighter planes and helicopters, and unmanned aircraft such as remotely piloted vehicles (RPVs), which are controlled from a distance, and unmanned aerial vehicles (UAVs), which are computer-guided to preprogrammed targets. Iraq, for example, developed a drop tank for spraying anthrax weapons that could be attached to either a piloted fighter plane or a UAV. The tank was designed to spray up to two thousand liters (2113 quarts) of anthrax on a target.

Scientists warn, though, that anthrax bacteria may be destroyed in the explosion of an artillery shell, bomb, or warhead. Some experts suggest, therefore, that spraying anthrax spores from a low-flying airplane—like a crop duster equipped with nozzles that produce a fine cloud of particles—would be the best means of spreading the disease. Likely targets for such an attack might include cities, major seaports, and military bases.

Simpler means of dispersing anthrax, which terrorist groups might use, include putting spores into food or water; placing spores in letters or packages; pouring spores into power sprayers mounted on cars, trucks, or boats; or loading spores into handheld sprayers for distribution in subway systems, shopping malls, sports arenas, airports, commercial buildings, government complexes, and so on.

The unmanned Global Hawk aircraft can fly great distances at incredible speed. Terrorists could use similar aircraft to disperse anthrax bioweapons.

U.S. AIR FORCE

Risks Associated with Anthrax Weapons

Though many countries and terrorist organizations are suspected of having anthrax weapons, they may be reluctant to deploy them. There are several reasons for this. First, anthrax may not spread as expected because of unsuitable weather conditions or barriers in the terrain, such as hills, valleys, forests, and so on. Second, anthrax microbes do not have immediate effects. Thus, in time of war, soldiers could continue to fight until they became too ill. Third, the spread of anthrax cannot be guided. Hence, the disease might strike the people that release it. This phenomenon, called "the boomerang effect," was observed during World War II. In 1942, after Japan dispersed germ weapons over one Chinese province, more than seventeen hundred Japanese soldiers were infected and killed. And lastly, nations that release biological weapons might expect catastrophic retaliation from the enemy.

Nevertheless, military experts in developed nations fear that their enemies might use biological weapons. Thus, the United States and its allies are studying ways to detect anthrax and other bioweapons, and to protect people from them.

Chapter 5

Detecting and Responding to Anthrax Bioweapons

O N September 18, 2001—a week after the September 11 al-Qaeda terrorist attacks on the Pentagon and World Trade Center—letters containing anthrax spores were sent to Tom Brokaw at NBC news, Peter Jennings at ABC news, Dan Rather at CBS news, and to the editor of the *New York Post.* The letters passed through a mail-sorting facility in Hamilton, New Jersey. Two employees at the *New York Post,* two NBC workers, an employee at CBS, six local postal workers, and a baby who had visited ABC all became ill. The illnesses were not immediately recognized as anthrax, but the victims received medical treatment and recovered.

Two weeks later, in early October 2001, Robert Stevens—a photo editor at the *Sun* (a tabloid newsmagazine) in Boca Raton, Florida—died from an undiagnosed disease. Two other employees in the building also fell ill but were treated and recuperated. The illnesses were later identified as anthrax, and *Bacillus anthracis* spores were traced to a mail bin in the building.

Soon afterward, in mid-October, anthrax-spore-containing letters were sent to Senator Tom Daschle of South Dakota and Senator Patrick Leahy of Vermont, who work in the Senate office buildings in Washington, D.C. On October 17 anthrax spores were also found in mail bins at the House of Representatives in Washington, D.C. The Capitol Hill buildings were closed for cleaning, and hundreds of congressional workers were told to start taking the antibiotic ciprofloxacin to protect them from anthrax.

The mailed anthrax spores were examined by scientists at the U.S. Army Medical Research Institute of Infectious Disease (USAMRIID) at Fort Detrick, Maryland. The experts found that the anthrax powder in the Senate letters was "professionally done" and "energetic,"[41] meaning that the spores wafted into the air to form a spreading cloud. This is a characteristic of weaponized anthrax. In addition, scientists discovered that the strain of anthrax in the letters was identical to a strain being studied at USAMRIID.

Moreover, researchers found that though the letters were tightly sealed and taped, the anthrax spores were small enough to squeeze through pores in the envelopes when the letters passed through mail-sorting machines. Government investigators believe, therefore, that the terrorist (or terrorists) had not meant to infect postal workers or the general public. Nevertheless, in October 2001 five postal workers in Washington, D.C., fell ill. Joseph P. Curseen Jr. and Thomas L. Morris Jr., who worked at the Brentwood mail-sorting

Traces of anthrax spores were found on this anonymous letter sent to Vermont senator Patrick Leahy in 2001.

facility in Washington, D.C., developed inhalation anthrax and died. The other victims in Washington, D.C., were treated and survived. The Brentwood postal facility was closed soon afterward, and two thousand postal workers were instructed to start taking antibiotics.

About two weeks later, on October 31, a New York City hospital worker named Kathy Nguyen died of inhalation anthrax. She did not work or live near a building where anthrax had been found, and no one knows how she contracted the disease. A similar incident occurred on November 30, when Ottilie Lundgren, a Connecticut resident, died of inhalation anthrax. Researchers speculated that the women may have handled mail that passed through an anthrax-contaminated postal facility.

When law enforcement officials realized the United States was in the midst of an anthrax attack, the Federal Bureau of Investigation (FBI) obtained and analyzed the four anthrax letters that had been found (though more were apparently mailed). The September 2001 letters sent to news outlets in New York City read:

09-11-01
THIS IS NEXT
TAKE PENACILIN NOW
DEATH TO AMERICA
DEATH TO ISRAEL
ALLAH IS GREAT [42]

The October 2001 letters mailed to senators in Washington, D.C., said:

09-11-01
YOU CAN NOT STOP US.
WE HAVE THIS ANTHRAX.
YOU DIE NOW.
ARE YOU AFRAID?
DEATH TO AMERICA.
DEATH TO ISRAEL.
ALLAH IS GREAT. [43]

After a massive investigation FBI profilers concluded that the anthrax terrorist was a white, American, male scientist associated

Source: CNN website (www.cnn.com)/Associated Press/University of Arizona.

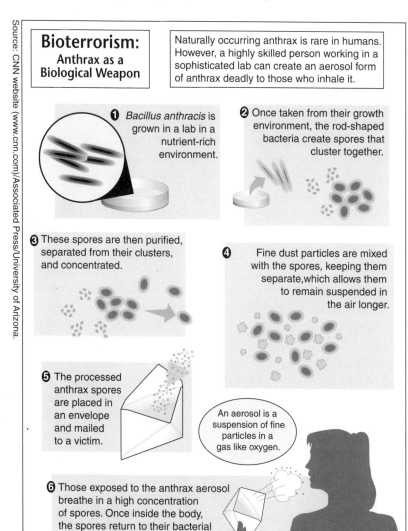

Bioterrorism:
Anthrax as a Biological Weapon

Naturally occurring anthrax is rare in humans. However, a highly skilled person working in a sophisticated lab can create an aerosol form of anthrax deadly to those who inhale it.

❶ *Bacillus anthracis* is grown in a lab in a nutrient-rich environment.

❷ Once taken from their growth environment, the rod-shaped bacteria create spores that cluster together.

❸ These spores are then purified, separated from their clusters, and concentrated.

❹ Fine dust particles are mixed with the spores, keeping them separate, which allows them to remain suspended in the air longer.

❺ The processed anthrax spores are placed in an envelope and mailed to a victim.

An aerosol is a suspension of fine particles in a gas like oxygen.

❻ Those exposed to the anthrax aerosol breathe in a high concentration of spores. Once inside the body, the spores return to their bacterial state, causing a toxic, and often deadly, anthrax infection.

with USAMRIID or another U.S. bioweapons laboratory. Experts suspected that the culprit had dated the letters "09-11-01," and included the phrases "Death to America" and "Allah is Great" to cast suspicion on Arabs.

Eventually, the FBI identified Steven Hatfill, a scientist and former bioweapons researcher at USAMRIID, as a "person of interest" (suspect) in the investigation. However, after two years Hatfill had not been arrested, and in September 2003 the scientist filed a lawsuit against the Justice Department, claiming it had violated his constitutional rights and damaged his reputation. No other suspects in the anthrax attacks were identified, and the case remains unsolved.

Though tragedy resulted from the 2001 anthrax attacks, the damage was minor compared to what might have happened if there had been a massive bioterrorist assault. Moreover, development of biological weapons and terrorist activity has increased alarmingly since the close of World War II. Thus, the United States and its allies have been taking steps to protect themselves from anthrax and other bioweapons.

The Danger of Anthrax Attacks

Military experts have become especially fearful of state-sponsored terrorist organizations. William C. Patrick, who developed anthrax bioweapons at Fort Detrick, Maryland, remarks, "I don't think

This computer illustration graphically depicts how an aerosol anthrax spray could be used against a city in a biological weapons attack.

that Tom, Dick, and Harry terrorists, without significant train-
ing and experience . . . could develop an agent that would cause
serious harm to this country. My biggest concern now is a rogue
country that supports state terrorism and has the facilities to prepare, for example, a good dry powder of anthrax."[44] Patrick spec-
ulates that terrorist organizations might disperse anthrax powder
in buildings and subway systems, causing serious harm to American civilians.

Because of the danger of anthrax attacks, the United States has
been seeking ways to protect its population from *Bacillus anthracis*
and other bioweapons. Military officials believe an anthrax attack
would probably involve the release of anthrax spores in the form
of a spray, called "aerosolized anthrax," that could spread quickly.
The Working Group on Civilian Biodefense, an expert panel as-
sembled by the Center for Civilian Biodefense Studies at the Johns
Hopkins University Bloomberg School of Public Health, notes that
aerosolized anthrax could be widely dispersed within a few hours
to one day. Thus, there would be little time to destroy the spores
or provide antibiotics to affected populations. Moreover,
aerosolized anthrax is invisible. Therefore, the first evidence of an
anthrax strike might be large numbers of people with flulike illnesses that rapidly develop into inhalation anthrax—the most
deadly form of the disease.

To prevent such an occurrence, U.S. officials believe the nation
needs fast-working, dependable, low-cost microbe detectors. In
the event of an anthrax strike, such devices could "sound an
alarm," allowing exposed individuals to be treated immediately.
James Woolsey, former director of the U.S. Central Intelligence
Agency, comments: "With [an] anthrax [attack] there is a period of
one to two days before people become symptomatic, when almost
all of the people who had been exposed could be treated and
treated successfully. If one . . . had the right types of sensors so that
you knew that a biological attack had occurred . . . you could save
a vast share of lives."[45]

At this time, the United States does not have such germ detectors. However, scientists in government, industry, and universities are looking for ways to develop them.

Bacteriophage Detectors

Researchers at the Center for Environmental Biotechnology (CEB) at the University of Tennessee are developing a germ detector that uses bacteriophage (bacteria-killing viruses) to detect microbes. Scientists at the CEB are creating bacteriophage that give off light when they infect certain bacteria, such as *Bacillus anthracis*. For example, when a prepared bacteriophage infects an anthrax organism, a device called a luminescent bioreporter that is incorporated into the bacteriophage emits light rays. The light is detected by a tiny photodetector contained in a microchip, which gives off a signal that is sent to a desktop computer. The tiny detection device, composed of the bacteriophage attached to the microchip, is called a microluminometer.

According to the inventors, microluminometers would be inexpensive detectors that could identify microbes instantly. Moreover, microluminometers could be used almost anywhere. Steven Ripp, senior research specialist at CEB, notes: "You could just toss them into air vents or water samples." In addition to activating the light signal, the bacteriophage would kill the microbes. "Since the phage are infecting the pathogen [disease-causing organism], they're ultimately killing it as well," observes Ripp. "So the phage itself could be sprayed onto an infected area to render the pathogens harmless."[46] Sample microluminometers are now being tested. The inventors note, however, that an efficient microluminometer against anthrax may take years to develop.

Nucleic Acid Analyzer

Researchers at Lawrence Livermore National Laboratory (LLNL) in California have been developing a device that detects microbes such as anthrax bacteria by means of their genetic material, composed of compounds called nucleic acids. Using anthrax as an example, the process works as follows: First, the investigators map the genetic material of the *Bacillus anthracis* bacteria. The scientists then make artificial pieces of DNA that will bind to the anthrax organism's genetic material. When the human-made DNA and the anthrax organism's genetic material unite, a bit of fluorescent dye is released from the artificial DNA. With the proper lighting, the fluorescent

U.S. researchers are developing a way to detect the presence of anthrax and other microbes using strands of DNA.

dye glows. Theoretically, artificial segments of DNA matched to *Bacillus anthracis* could be used in anthrax detection devices. A "glowing reaction" would signal the presence of anthrax bacteria.

By 2001 LLNL scientists had fashioned a microbe detector that could identify germs in seven to ten minutes and is small enough to fit into a handheld device or the pants pocket of some special forces uniforms. Called a Handheld Advanced Nucleic Acid Analyzer (HANAA), the apparatus has been tested at various sites, including the Food and Drug Administration, the Centers for Disease Control and Prevention in Atlanta, and Los Angeles County's emergency operations office. However, Pat Fitch, who heads the team developing the microbe detector, notes that setting up the device is a "non-trivial [complicated] exercise,"[47] and that HANAA requires a highly trained operator to process samples.

Microbial Biosensors

Christopher Woolverton at Kent State University in Ohio and his colleagues at Northeastern Ohio University's College of Medicine and Kent State's Liquid Crystal Institute have also designed a hand-held germ detector, called a microbial biosensor. MicroDiagnosis, a Washington State company, is marketing the device.

A scientist demonstrates a device he developed for detecting anthrax and other organic material hidden in sealed containers. Such devices could be lifesavers.

Woolverton's microbial biosensors have been successfully tested on several microorganisms, and an anthrax version is being developed. It will work like this: The microbial biosensor contains a liquid crystal layer that blocks light. Anthrax organisms, when present, combine with specific antibodies (substances that attack germs) in the device. The anthrax-antibody clusters disrupt the liquid crystal layer, allowing light to pass through. The light is detected by an optical scanner that sends a signal to a small computer. According to the developers, the microbial biosensor will be able to detect anthrax germs in about five minutes.

Biological Integrated Detection System

For some time, the U.S. military has had a relatively crude, bulky microbe detector, meant to be used on the battlefield. The apparatus, which looks like a small house with three chimneys, is called the Biological Integrated Detection System (BIDS). Mounted on a Humvee vehicle, BIDS uses a number of technologies to detect biological organisms, including bioluminescence (the production of light by living organisms), flow cytometry (identification of organisms by light-absorbing or fluorescing properties), mass spectrometry (weight determination), and immunological assays (using antibodies to identify organisms). BIDS, which can identify a broad range of microorganisms, requires two expert operators and takes forty-five minutes to complete an analysis.

Scientists at LLNL and Los Alamos National Laboratory in New Mexico have developed a more compact microbe detector, about the size of an automated teller machine (ATM). The device is designed to be used in locations like airports, sports arenas, and convention centers. The apparatus, which analyzes air samples within one hour, can report the presence of anthrax and other deadly germs.

The U.S. government hopes to develop a more efficient germ detector, connected to a remote-controlled vehicle. The new device, called a point detector, would "sniff" air samples. Within fifteen minutes the detector would determine if any of twenty-six dangerous microbes, including anthrax bacteria, was present. This new invention, however, may take years to perfect.

Veterinary Alerts

Because rapid, easy-to-use detection devices for deadly microbes are not yet available, the U.S. government uses other means to monitor dangerous germs. One method involves a network of veterinarians. The federal government trains veterinarians, recruited by county and state health departments across the nation, to recognize animal illnesses that could indicate a biological attack.

In the case of anthrax, for example, a bioweapons strike would probably affect animals as well as people. Thus, veterinarians might be among the first doctors to see the disease. This is especially true because small animals like cats and dogs have relatively fast metabolisms. They could, therefore, be among the first victims to display anthrax symptoms. Jean Feldman, a veterinarian who specializes in treating horses, cattle, sheep, and goats, observes: "Pets could be the sentinels of a bioterrorism attack. . . . Certain diseases would be unusual in dogs and cats and if they show up, vets should think that there may have been a deliberate infection and notify the appropriate public health and veterinarian authorities of it." [48] Federal authorities hope that veterinarians, along with farmers, ranchers, and other people that work with animals, might function as an "early warning system" if an anthrax strike occurs.

Preparations for a Possible Anthrax Attack

In spring 1998 New York City officials conducted simulated anthrax attacks as part of the DoD's Domestic Preparedness Program, established by a 1996 act of Congress. Under this program, the U.S. Army's Chemical and Biological Defense Command (CBDC) is helping city and state governments prepare for a terrorist attack. Suzanne Fournier, a spokeswoman for the CBDC, explains: "We're using New York City as a special city to work on biological incidents. . . . I can't give a lot of specifics, but you actually have the response teams go out and act out what they would do. . . . You also have a person playing a terrorist acting out what he would do." [49] The exercise demonstrated that a bioterrorist attack in New York could be devastating. Consequently, New York officials drew up plans, usable in many urban areas, to prepare for a biological weapons strike.

New York firefighters practice a biological weapons attack drill in 2003. An actual attack could be devastating on a very large scale.

Jerome Hauer, New York City's emergency management director, describes steps the city has taken to deal with a germ weapon attack. First, to detect a sudden increase in the number of sick residents, New York monitors hospital admissions, emergency room visits, unusual deaths, and sales of over-the-counter medications. Second, the city has established many "points of distribution" for dispensing drugs in an emergency. Third, New York has taught large numbers of doctors, nurses, police, firefighters, and other emergency workers what to do during a germ weapon emergency. And last, New York stockpiled large quantities of medication for immediate treatment of bioterrorism victims.

In addition to New York, the Domestic Preparedness Program— now under the jurisdiction of the Department of Justice—has helped Baltimore and other cities develop plans to deal with bioweapon attacks. The program trains various kinds of emergency workers to detect deadly microbes, furnish medical treatment, decontaminate affected areas, and provide law enforcement in a crisis situation.

To minimize the devastation an anthrax attack might cause, the U.S. government is also sponsoring the development of new and better human anthrax vaccines.

Future Anthrax Vaccines

Misgivings about the safety and efficiency of the currently used anthrax vaccine, MDPH-AVA, as well as the large number of injections required for immunity, have stimulated research into alternative human anthrax vaccines. Since the 1980s U.S. scientists have been trying to develop either a purer cell-free vaccine or a live-organism vaccine. Their aim is to produce a vaccine that requires only one or two shots, has few adverse effects, and provides protection against all strains of anthrax. Several live-organism anthrax vaccines have been tested, but the United States has not yet approved any for use in people.

More recently, in the 1990s, scientists started researching experimental vaccines called "gene vaccines." These vaccines are composed of a mixture of genes (genetic material) from different bacteria. Researchers at Maxygen, a company in Redwood, California, are trying to develop two gene vaccines using a procedure called "gene shuffling." In the past, Maxygen mixed up thousands of genes from various microorganisms to produce an enzyme, used in laundry detergents, that dissolves grass stains. Maxygen hopes to make an even stronger enzyme that can dissolve anthrax organisms. Maxygen is also researching another gene vaccine that would stimulate a huge immune response. They hope this will induce "superimmunity" to anthrax bacteria.

Vical, a vaccine producer in San Diego, California, is also researching gene vaccines. In 2003 Vical announced that it had successfully used a gene vaccine to protect rabbits from anthrax. Vical plans to experiment on another animal species, then move on to human trials. The company hopes to develop a human anthrax vaccine that will require just two injections.

In the early 2000s another pharmaceutical company, DynPort, in Frederick, Maryland, developed an anthrax vaccine that acts faster than MDPH-AVA. DynPort hopes to market the vaccine after human clinical trials are completed.

Vaccine producers are also studying the possibility of producing aerosol vaccines, which would be inhaled. These vaccines could be sprayed over many square miles, providing rapid protection to a large population.

In addition to creating new vaccines, scientists are also developing new medicines to treat people who come in contact with anthrax.

Broad Spectrum Medical Defense

During an interview in 2001, Ken Alibek, an anthrax expert, was asked how the United States could best defend itself against biological weapons. Alibek replied that, in his opinion, vaccines did not provide the best protection. He notes that broad spectrum medications (medicines that work against many microbes) would work better. "There are too many biological agents that could be used in biological weapons," observes Alibek. "It is impossible to imagine how to develop this number of vaccines. . . . The best approach is to develop a broad spectrum medical defense."[50] Alibek is researching broad spectrum medicines and hopes to develop them within five years.

Other medical researchers are also searching for new ways to treat anthrax, because disease-causing microorganisms like *Bacillus anthracis* can become resistant to commonly used medications.

Investigating New Treatments

A number of scientists and pharmaceutical companies in the United States are searching for ways to improve the nation's defenses against anthrax and other infectious diseases. Beginning in the early 2000s, U.S. legislators planned to fund these efforts through Project Bioshield. This program provides money for the federal government to purchase large quantities of vaccines and medicines to fight potential bioterrorism.

Anacor Pharmaceuticals, a company in Palo Alto, California, is conducting animal trials for new antibiotics to treat anthrax. However, antibiotics—which work by killing bacteria—cannot eliminate *Bacillus anthracis* toxins from the human body. Moreover, no currently available medication can counteract anthrax toxins. For

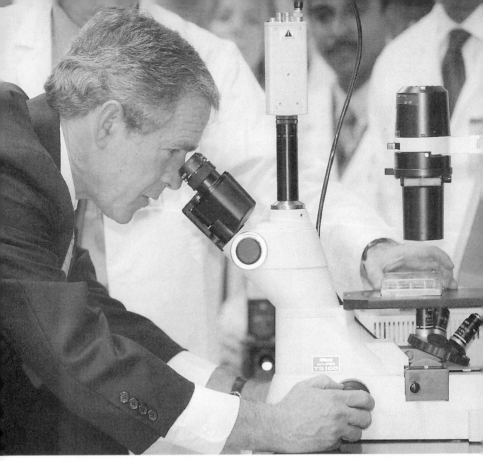

President Bush examines firsthand the results of recent research on bioweapons protection. The federal government funds such research through Project Bioshield.

this reason, scientists have been trying to develop two new medications for treating anthrax victims. One new medicine would prevent the formation of anthrax toxins. The other new treatment, an antitoxin, would neutralize anthrax toxins that are already present. The U.S.-based company Human Genome Sciences Incorporated (HGSI) has developed a new type of antibody drug, called Abthrax, that counteracts anthrax toxins. HGSI has successfully tested the medicine on animals and hopes to begin human trials soon. According to HGSI, a single dose of Abthrax, administered soon after exposure, might protect a person from anthrax; and Abthrax could also be used to safeguard firefighters and police who enter contaminated buildings, soldiers exposed to anthrax bioweapons, or civilians after a terrorist attack.

Medical researchers have also been studying the possibility of using bacteriophage (viruses that kill bacteria) to control anthrax infections. In the laboratory, bacteriophage have been able to kill *Bacillus anthracis* cells as well as germinating spores. Scientists believe that someday these viruses may provide a new treatment for anthrax. Taking steps to avoid contact with biological weapons is another defense recommended by some bioterrorism experts.

Safe Rooms

U.S. senator Bill Frist is a physician as well as an authority on bioterrorism. Frist recommends that every American home have a "safe room" where families can stay in the event of an attack

A government official explains to members of the press the specifications of a safe room, designed to provide protection from a bioterror attack.

with a bioweapon like anthrax. According to Frist, a safe room should be windowless, have a strong door, and contain a radio, telephone, medical supplies, and food and water to last several days. Other useful supplies include flashlights, cell phones, and facemasks with filters. Koken Ltd., a Japanese company that makes hazard masks, recently developed a child-size version to be used against biological weapons. Fumikazu Tanaka, a manager at the company, notes: "With the [terrorist] attacks . . . and the anthrax scare, people began to get nervous . . . and for parents, a priority is to protect their children." [51] In Frist's opinion, every family should be prepared "when, not if, America is hit by another biological attack . . . like [the] anthrax scare [of 2001]." [52]

Aerial Spraying to Kill Anthrax Spores

One method of counteracting an attack with aerosolized anthrax would be to destroy the anthrax spores. Fearing bioterrorist attacks on the United States for many years, Mitch Fadem, a scientist at Kent State University, has been studying ways to kill airborne spores. "I've been telling people for a long time it [bioterrorism] is going to happen here," observes Fadem. "The climate was right. I knew how open the United States was and how easy it would be to get the materials." [53]

Fadem's background in toxicology (the study of poisonous substances) led him to think of using chemicals to kill *Bacillus anthracis*. The scientist tested an antimicrobial foam pesticide that can destroy anthrax spores. The pesticide, invented by Sandia National Laboratories, is composed of two disinfectants: alkyl dimethyl benzyl ammonium chloride and concentrated hydrogen peroxide. Fadem tested the foam in his laboratory to find concentrations that would destroy anthrax spores without harming people or property.

Fadem plans to use low-flying military airplanes during field trials to spray the toxic foam over areas contaminated with nondeadly organisms, such as *Bacillus globigii,* that are similar to anthrax germs. If Fadem succeeds, this method may be used to neutralize aerosolized anthrax in the future.

Defense Against Anthrax Attacks

The anthrax-letter attacks of 2001 demonstrated the terror and damage the disease can cause in the wrong hands. It also demonstrated that better methods of detection and treatment are needed to effectively combat the disease in the event it is used as a weapon by rogue nations or terrorists. Scientists are devising a number of promising new technologies to counter the anthrax threat and hope to be able to deploy them in the next few years. If they are successful, the result will be a safer world.

Notes

Introduction: A Deadly Disease

1. Homer, *The Iliad*, Book I, Internet Classics Archives. http://classics. mit.edu/Homer/iliad.html.
2. Virgil, *The Georgics*, Georgic III, Internet Classics Archives. http://classics.mit.edu/Virgil/georgics.html.

Chapter 1: Anthrax in Animals

3. David Thain, "State Veterinarian Reports Anthrax Outbreak," College of Agriculture, Biotechnology, and Natural Resources, University of Nevada, Reno, August 16, 2000. www.ag.unr. edu.
4. Quoted in Ken Ringle, "The Ancient History of a Bacterium: Anthrax Scares Go Way Back," *Washington Post,* October 27, 2001. www.washingtonpost.com.
5. Quoted in Guy Gugliotta, "Anthrax Has Inspired Dread and Breakthroughs," *Washington Post,* November 5, 2001. www.ph. ucla.edu.
6. Quoted in Steve Hill, "Anthrax Vaccinations Suggested After Increase in Cases," *AgNews,* August 15, 1997. http://agnews. tamu.edu.
7. Quoted in G. Bruckner et al., "Chapter 1. Socio-Economic Consequences for Poor Livestock Farmers of Animal Diseases and VPH Problems," Food and Agriculture Organization of the United Nations, 2003. www.fao.org.
8. Quoted in Crusoe Osagie, "Invest in Animal Health Research to Alleviate Poverty," This Day on the Web, January 14, 2003. www.this dayonline.com.

Chapter 2: A Human Scourge

9. Quoted in Michael S. James, "Cattle and Other Grazing Animals Appear Most at Risk During Wild Anthrax Outbreaks," ABC News, November 2, 2001. http://abcnews.go.com.

10. Quoted in Analysis and Perspective, "Thousands Around the World Infected Every Year with Natural Anthrax," Attack on America, November 11, 2001. http://multimedia.belointeractive.com.

11. Thira Sirisanthana and Arthur E. Brown, "Anthrax of the Gastrointestinal Tract," *Emerging Infectious Diseases*, July 2002. www.cdc.gov.

12. Quoted in David M. Morens, "Epidemic Anthrax in the Eighteenth Century, the Americas," *Emerging Infectious Diseases*, 2002. www.cdc.gov.

Chapter 3: Preventing and Treating Anthrax

13. Quoted in Hill, "Anthrax Vaccinations Suggested After Increase in Cases."

14. Quoted in Michael Schommer and Bill Hartmann, "State Veterinarian Urges Northwestern Minnesota Livestock Producers to Consider Anthrax Vaccinations for Their Grazing Cattle," Minnesota Board of Animal Health, June 26, 2002. www.bah.state.mn.us.

15. Quoted in James, "Cattle and Other Grazing Animals Appear Most at Risk During Wild Anthrax Outbreaks."

16. Quoted in Tom Montgomery, "Anthrax!—The Ilkley Connection," *Village Tidings on the Web*, Spring 2002. http://pages.britishlibrary.net/village.tidings/spr_02/page24.html.

17. Meryl Nass, "Anthrax Vaccine Safety and Efficacy," Quik Internet, Anthrax Vaccine Links and Information, January 2, 1998. www.dallasnw.quik.com.

18. Meryl Nass, "Biological Warfare and Vaccines: Anthrax," *ASA Newsletter*, 2000. www.asanltr.com.

19. Quoted in Dave Eberhart, "Dr. Meryl Nass: On the Front Lines of the Anthrax Vaccine Wars," *Stars and Stripes*, March 5, 2001. www.majorbates.com.

20. Peter C.B. Turnbull, "Anthrax Vaccines: Past, Present, and Future," *Vaccine*, 1991. www.anthrax.mil.

21. Meryl Nass, "Anthrax Vaccine Not Safe and Effective," *Emergency Medicine News*, Alliance for Human Research Protection, July 18, 2002. www.researchprotection.org.

22. Quoted in Timothy W. Maier, "GAO: Shots Led to Military Attrition," *Insight on the News*, November 14, 2002. www.insightmag.com.

23. Quoted in Nass, "Anthrax Vaccine Safety and Efficacy."

24. Nass, "Anthrax Vaccine Safety and Efficacy."

Chapter 4: Anthrax Biological Weapons

25. Quoted in Edward M. Eitzen Jr. and Ernest T. Takafuji, "Historical Overview of Biological Warfare," Borden Institute, Walter Reed Army Medical Center, *Textbook of Military Medicine: Medical Aspects of Chemical and Biological Warfare*, 2003. www.nbc-med.org.

26. Quoted in Robert Harris and Jeremy Paxman, *A Higher Form of Killing: The Secret Story of Chemical and Biological Warfare.* New York: Hill and Wang, 1982, p. 70.

27. Quoted in *Frontline*, "Interview: James Woolsey," PBS, 1998. www.pbs.org.

28. Quoted in *Frontline*, "Interview: James Woolsey."

29. Quoted in *Frontline*, "Interview: James Woolsey."

30. Quoted in Seymour M. Hersh, *Chemical and Biological Warfare: America's Hidden Arsenal.* New York: Bobbs-Merrill, 1968, pp. 16–17.

31. Quoted in Harris and Paxman, *A Higher Form of Killing,* p. 73.

32. Quoted in Federation of American Scientists, "The U.S. Government's Interpretation of the Biological and Toxins Weapons Convention," A Report of the Working Group on Biological Weapons, November 2002. www.fas.org.

33. Quoted in Alexandra M. Lord, "A Brief History of Anthrax," Office of the Public Health Service, Lister Hill National Center for Biomedical Communications, December 2001. http://lhncbc.nlm.nih.gov.

34. Quoted in Lord, "A Brief History of Anthrax."

35. Barbara Hatch Rosenberg, "Anthrax Attacks Pushed Open an Ominous Door," Federation of American Scientists, September 22, 2002. www.fas.org.

36. Quoted in *Nova*, "Bioterror: Interviews with Biowarriors Bill Patrick and Ken Alibek," PBS, November 2001. www.pbs.org.

37. Quoted in *Nova*, "Bioterror."

38. Quoted in RAmEx Ars Medica, Inc., "Anthrax, Made in the USA," *Today in Vidyya*, April 2, 2003. http://216.86.213.73/today/v3i209_5.htm.

39. Quoted in Mike Nartker, "Japan: Aum Shinrikyo Released Harmless Anthrax in 1993," *Global Security Newswire*, February 21, 2003. www.nti.org.

40. Quoted in Hersh, *Chemical and Biological Warfare*, p. 85.

Chapter 5: Detecting and Responding to Anthrax Bioweapons

41. Quoted in Richard Preston, *The Demon in the Freezer*. New York: Random House, 2002, p. 72.

42. Quoted in Ed Lake, "The Anthrax Cases," July 30, 2003. www.anthraxinvestigation.com.

43. Quoted in Lake "The Anthrax Cases."

44. Quoted in *Nova*, "Bioterror."

45. Quoted in *Frontline*, "Interview: James Woolsey."

46. Quoted in Elise LeQuire, "The Assault on Anthrax: Genetically Engineered Bacteria Created by UT Researchers May Join the Fight Against Bioterrorism," *InSites*, Winter 2001. http://eerc.ra.utk.edu.

47. Quoted in Jeffrey M. Perkel, "Probing What's Out There: A Marriage of Molecular Biology and Classic Microbiology Yields New Techniques for Biosensing, Epidemiology, and Microbial Diversity Studies," *Scientist*, May 5, 2003. www.the-scientist.com.

48. Quoted in Jeff Shields, "Vets Trained to Spot Animal Symptoms of Biological/Chemical Attacks," *Philadelphia Inquirer*, April 9, 2003. www.philly.com.

49. Quoted in *New Scientist* Articles on BioTerrorism, "Nowhere to Hide—America Is Waking Up to the Threat of Bioterrorism, but Is There Any Real Defense?" March 21, 1998. http://members.rogers.com.

50. Quoted in *Nova*, "Bioterror."

51. Quoted in Reuters, "Firm Launches Kids' Masks for Bio-Warfare," Miscellaneous Anthrax Articles—Part I, April 3, 2002. http://anthraxinvestigation.com.

52. Quoted in Reuters, "Senate's Doctor Prescribes Biowar Safe Room," Miscellaneous Anthrax Articles—Part I, April 13, 2002. http://anthraxinvestigation.com.

53. Quoted in Katie Byard, "Kent State Researchers Hope for Federal Aid for Counterterrorism," Miscellaneous Anthrax Articles—Part I, April 3, 2002. http://anthraxinvestigation.com.

Glossary

autoimmune diseases: Illnesses that occur when the body's immune system attacks its own tissues.

biological weapons: Bacteria, viruses, or toxic substances produced by living organisms, used to intentionally harm plants, animals, or humans.

capsule: A gel or slime layer that covers the surface of some bacteria; when present on disease-causing organisms, it makes them more deadly.

edema: Swelling caused by an abnormal accumulation of fluid in the body tissues.

enzyme: A protein molecule that assists and speeds up chemical reactions.

fluorescence: The emission of light from a substance in response to radiation (such as light) from an outside source.

formaldehyde: A chemical substance used as an antiseptic, disinfectant, and preservative for living tissues.

germinate: To sprout or begin to grow.

immune system: The body system that defends the body against infection, disease, and foreign substances.

nonvirulent microorganisms: Organisms that are unable to cause disease or injury.

septicemia: A systemic disease caused by the presence of deadly microorganisms or their toxins in the blood; also called blood poisoning.

spore: A hardy, resistant form of a bacterial organism, produced in response to unfavorable environmental conditions.

strain: A specific variety of plant, animal, or microorganism.

unencapsulated bacteria: Bacteria that lack a capsule.

virulent microorganisms: Organisms that are able to cause disease or injury.

zoonotic disease: Disease of nonhuman animals that may be transmitted to humans.

Organizations to Contact

The American Veterinary Medical Association (AVMA)
1931 N. Meacham Rd., Suite 100
Schaumburg, IL 60173
(847) 925-8070
avmainfo@avma.org
www.avma.org

AVMA provides veterinarians, ranchers, farmers, and pet owners comprehensive information on animal care and animal diseases.

Anthrax Vaccine Immunization Program (AVIP)
1-877-GET-VACC (1-877-438-8222)
AVIP@otsg.amedd.army.mil (for questions or issues concerning
    vaccination)
www.anthrax.osd.mil

AVIP offers general information about forms of anthrax in humans, anthrax as a biological weapon, and the safety of human anthrax vaccine.

Centers for Disease Control and Prevention (CDC)
1600 Clifton Rd.
Atlanta, GA 30333
(404) 639-3311
www.cdc.gov

CDC offers extensive information about epidemic diseases and public health issues.

United States Department of Agriculture (USDA)
1400 Independence Ave. SW
Washington, DC 20250
(202) 720-2791
www.usda.gov

The USDA offers comprehensive information about farming, agricultural services, and diseases of domestic animals.

For Further Reading

Books

Herbert M. Levine, *Chemical and Biological Weapons in Our Times.*
New York: Franklin Watts, 2000. A discussion of chemical and
biological weapons, including their use, guarding against
them, emergency responsiveness, and attempts to control
them.

Richard Preston, *The Demon in the Freezer.* New York: Random
House, 2002. A discussion of current threats from biological
weapons, including information about the anthrax terror letters
of 2001 and Dr. Ken Alibek's development of anthrax weapons
for the former Soviet Union.

Laurence Pringle, *Chemical and Biological Warfare: The Cruelest
Weapons.* Berkeley Heights, NJ: Enslow, 2000. A discussion of
chemical and biological weapons, including their history, development, proliferation, defenses against them, and bioterrorism.

Brian Solomon, ed., *Chemical and Biological Warfare.* New York: H.W.
Wilson, 1999. A discussion of chemical and biological weapons,
including their history, threatened use by Saddam Hussein, vaccination of the U.S. military, and increasing threats from germ
weapons.

Periodical

Richard Lacayo, "Will We Be Safer?" *Time,* September 8, 2003.

Internet Sources

Frontline, "Interview: James Woolsey," PBS, 1998. www.pbs.org.

Guy Gugliotta, "Anthrax Has Inspired Dread and Breakthroughs,"
Washington Post, November 5, 2001. www.ph.ucla.edu.

Edwin M. Knights, "Anthrax," *History Magazine,* 2003. www.history-magazine.com.

Website

Centers for Disease Control and Prevention (www.cdc.gov). This website provides extensive news and information about public health issues and infectious diseases.

Works Consulted

Books

Bill Frist, *When Every Moment Counts: What You Need to Know About Bioterrorism from the Senate's Only Doctor.* Lanham, MD: Rowman & Littlefield, 2002. A discussion of biological weapons and the steps people can take to protect themselves against a biological attack.

Jeanne Guillemin, *Anthrax: The Investigation of a Deadly Outbreak.* Berkeley: University of California Press, 1999. A detailed description of the author's investigation of the anthrax outbreak that occurred in Sverdlovsk (in the former USSR) in 1979.

Robert Harris and Jeremy Paxman, *A Higher Form of Killing: The Secret Story of Chemical and Biological Warfare.* New York: Hill and Wang, 1982. A discussion of the development and use of chemical and biological weapons, including a detailed discussion of the British experiments with anthrax on Gruinard Island in the 1940s.

Seymour M. Hersh, *Chemical and Biological Warfare: America's Hidden Arsenal.* New York: Bobbs-Merrill, 1968. A discussion of chemical and biological warfare, including the history of biological warfare, attempts to control biological weapons, and endeavors to develop more potent bioweapons.

Judith Miller, Stephen Engelberg, and William Broad, *Biological Weapons and America's Secret War: Germs.* New York: Simon & Schuster, 2001. A discussion of the history of germ warfare, bioterrorist attacks with anthrax, anthrax vaccines, germ warfare protection, and biodefense weaknesses.

Internet Sources

H.P. Albarelli Jr., "The Secret History of Anthrax," WorldNetDaily.com, 2001. www.worldnetdaily.com.

Analysis and Perspective, "Thousands Around the World Infected Every Year with Natural Anthrax," Attack on America, November 11, 2001. http://multimedia.belointeractive.com.

Michael Barletta, Amy Sands, and Jonathan B. Tucker, "Keeping Track of Anthrax: The Case for a Biosecurity Convention," *Bulletin of the Atomic Scientists,* May/June 2002. www.the bulletin.org.

John Brookner, "Papers on Anthrax Collected by Dr J.H. Bell and Dr Fritz Eurich," Archives Hub of UK Universities and Colleges, December 4, 2001. www.archiveshub.ac.uk.

G. Bruckner et al., "Chapter 1. Socio-Economic Consequences for Poor Livestock Farmers of Animal Diseases and VPH Problems," Food and Agriculture Organization of the United Nations, 2003. www.fao.org.

Stephen Buckley, "Loss of Culturally Vital Cattle Leaves Dinka Tribe Adrift in Refugee Camps," *Washington Post,* August 24, 1997. www.washingtonpost.com.

Katie Byard, "Kent State Researchers Hope for Federal Aid for Counterterrorism," Miscellaneous Anthrax Articles—Part 1, April 3, 2002. http://anthraxinvestigation.com.

E. Ciftci, E. Ince, and U. Dogru, "Traditions, Anthrax, and Children," *Pediatric Dermatology,* Pub Med, January/February 2002. www.ncbi.nlm.nih.gov.

Jeff Clabaugh, "FDA Clears Anthrax Drug for Human Trials," *Washington Business Journal,* June 25, 2003. www.bizjournals.com.

Council on Foreign Relations, "The Anthrax Letters," Terrorism Questions and Answers, 2003. www.terrorismanswers.com.

Burke A. Cunha, "Anthrax," eMedicine, February 28, 2003. www. emedicine.com.

Vittorio Demicheli, Daniela Rivetti, Johnathan J. Deeks, Tom Jefferson, and Mark Pratt, "The Effectiveness and Safety of Vaccines Against Human Anthrax: A Systematic Review," *Vaccine,* 1998. www.anthrax.mil.

Devil's Brew Tables, "The Devil's Brew: Means of Delivery," Centre for Defence and International Security Studies, Lancaster University, 1996. www.cdiss.org.

Dave Eberhart, "Dr. Meryl Nass: On The Front Lines of the Anthrax Vaccine Wars," *Stars and Stripes,* March 5, 2001. www.major bates.com.

Edward M. Eitzen Jr. and Ernest T. Takafuji, "Historical Overview of Biological Warfare," Borden Institute, Walter Reed Army Medical Center, *Textbook of Military Medicine: Medical Aspects of Chemical and Biological Warfare*, 2003. www.nbc.med.org.

Emerging Infectious Diseases, "Clinical Issues in the Prophylaxis, Diagnosis, and Treatment of Anthrax," Conference Summary, January 4, 2002. www.cdc.gov.

Famine Early Warning System Network, "Southern Sudan: Food Security Report," FEWS NET, February 13, 2003. www.cip.ogp. noaa.gov.

Federation of American Scientists, "The U.S. Government's Interpretation of the Biological and Toxins Weapons Convention," A Report of the Working Group on Biological Weapons, November 2002. www.fas.org.

Tim Fison, "Some Ethnoveterinary Information from South Sudan," Vetwork UK, 2003. www.vetwork.org.uk.

Food and Agriculture Organization of the United Nations, "Anthrax: An Ancient Threat," News & Highlights, November 13, 2001. www.fao.org.

Mark Forbes, "Sailors Sent Home for Refusing Shots," *Vaccination Newsletter*, February 12, 2003. www.vaccinationnews.com.

Pat Hagan, "Anthrax Vaccine 'Safe,'" BBC News, March 20, 2003. http://news.bbc.co.uk.

Tom Hartley, "Veterinarians on Alert for Evidence of Bioterrorism," *Buffalo Business First*, May 5, 2003. www.bizjournals.com.

Erin Harty, "All About Anthrax," *VetCentric*, October 29, 2001. www. vetcentric.com.

Diedtra Henderson, "Japanese Cult Used Colorado Vaccine," *Denver Post*, February 17, 2003. www.cesnur.org.

Steve Hill, "Anthrax Vaccinations Suggested After Increase in Cases," *AgNews*, August 15, 1997. http://agnews.tamu.edu.

William Hoffman, "Louis Pasteur, Anthrax, and Bioterrorism," *The Doric Column*, October 22, 2001. http://mbbnet.umn.edu.

Homer, *The Iliad*, Internet Classics Archives. http://classics. mit.edu/Homer/iliad.html.

Michael S. James, "Cattle and Other Grazing Animals Appear Most at Risk During Wild Anthrax Outbreaks," ABC News, November 2, 2001. http://abcnews.go.com.

Bhushan Jayarao, Lawrence Hutchinson, David Wolfgang, and Robert Van Saun, "Anthrax: A Briefing for Veterinarians and Animal Health Professionals," Department of Veterinary Sciences, Penn State University, October, 2001. www.vetsci.psu.edu.

Wm. Robert Johnston, "Reports of Anthrax Bioattacks, September–October 2001," Johnston's Archive, October 27, 2001. www.johnstons archive.net.

F. Marc LaForce, "State-of-the-Art Clinical Article: Anthrax," *Clinical Infectious Diseases*, 1994. www.anthrax.mil.

A. Lahlou-Kass, "Biotechnology for Improved Livestock Productivity in Africa: The Challenges Ahead," ISNAR Biotechnology Service, April 1995. www.isnar.cgiar.org.

Ed Lake, "The Anthrax Cases," July 30, 2003. www.anthrax investigation.com.

Elise LeQuire, "The Assault on Anthrax: Genetically Engineered Bacteria Created by UT Researchers May Join the Fight Against Bioterrorism," *InSites*, Winter 2001. http://eerc.ra.utk.edu.

Lawrence Livermore National Laboratory, "Supercomputing Meets Future Needs," Newsline Special Insert, June 2003. www.llnl.gov.

Alexandra M. Lord, "A Brief History of Anthrax," Office of the Public Health Service, Lister Hill National Center for Biomedical Communications, December 2001. http://lhncbc.nlm.nih.gov.

Timothy W. Maier, "GAO: Shots Led to Military Attrition," *Insight on the News*, November 14, 2002. www.insightmag.com.

David Martin, "Traditional Medical Practitioners Seek International Recognition," Southern African News Features, November 16, 2001. www.sardc.net.

MDN Staff, "Liquid Crystals: Find Microbes at Lightning Speeds," *Medical Design News*, 2003. www.medicaldesignnews.com.

R.P. Misra, "Part 1: Production of Anthrax Spore Vaccine," FAO Animal Production and Health Paper 87, 1991. www.fao.org.

Tom Montgomery, "Anthrax!—The Ilkley Connection," *Village Tidings on the Web*, Spring 2002. http://pages.britishlibrary.net.

David M. Morens, "Epidemic Anthrax in the Eighteenth Century, the Americas," *Emerging Infectious Diseases*, 2002. www.cdc.gov.

Mike Nartker, "Japan: Aum Shinrikyo Released Harmless Anthrax in 1993," *Global Security Newswire*, February 21, 2003. www.nti.org.

Felicia Narvaez, "Nobelist Tells Med College Audience About Biological Warfare's History," Cornell News Service, November 4, 1999. www.news.cornell.edu.

Meryl Nass, "Anthrax Epizootic in Zimbabwe, 1978–1980: Due to Deliberate Spread?" Physicians for Social Responsibility, 1992. www.anthraxvaccine.org.

————, "Anthrax Vaccine Not Safe and Effective." *Emergency Medicine News,* Alliance for Human Research Protection, July 18, 2002. www.researchprotection.org.

————, "Anthrax Vaccine Safety and Efficacy," Quik Internet, Anthrax Vaccine Links and Information, January 2, 1998. www.dallasnw.quik.com.

————, "Biological Warfare and Vaccines: Anthrax," *ASA Newsletter,* 2000. www.asanltr.com.

J. Neumann, "Doc, I'd like to know more about Anthrax," *The Draft Horse Journal,* Winter 2001–02. www.drafthorsejournal.com.

New Scientist Articles on BioTerrorism, "Nowhere to Hide—America Is Waking Up to the Threat of Bioterrorism, but Is There Any Real Defense?" March 21, 1998. http://members.rogers.com.

Nova, "Bioterror: Interviews with Biowarriors Bill Patrick and Ken Alibek," PBS, November 2001. www.pbs.com.

Nova, "Interview with Biowarriors: Bill Patrick," PBS, November 2001. www.pbs.org.

Office of Pesticide Programs, "Decontamination Foam," U.S. Environmental Protection Agency, December 27, 2001. http://12.38.16.40.

Crusoe Osagie, "Invest in Animal Health Research to Alleviate Poverty," This Day on the Web, July 25, 2003. www.thisdayonline.com.

Jeffrey M. Perkel, "Probing What's Out There: A Marriage of Molecular Biology and Classic Microbiology Yields New Techniques for Biosensing, Epidemiology, and Microbial Diversity Studies," *Scientist,* May 5, 2003. www.the-scientist.com.

Kristen Philipkoski, "A Step Closer for Anthrax Vaccine," Wired News, March 10, 2003. www.wired.com.

John Pike, "M31E1 Biological Integrated Detection System (BIDS)," Global Security.org, January 31, 2003. www.globalsecurity.org.

James C. Pile, John D. Malone, Edward M. Eitzen, and Arthur M. Friedlander, "Anthrax as a Potential Biological Warfare Agent," *Archives of Internal Medicine*, 1998. http://archinte.ama-assn.org.

Dorothy Preslar, "Outbreak—Anthrax," Federation of American Scientists, October 2000. www.fas.org.

Christine Preston, "The Dinka of the Southern Sudan," Society and Culture Association, 2003. http://hsc.csu.edu.au.

Purina Mills Horse Health Section, "First Case of Animal Anthrax in 2003 Confirmed Near Del Rio," BarrelHorses.com, August 2003. http://barrelhorses.horsecity.com.

RAmEx Ars Medica, Inc., "Anthrax, Made in the USA," *Today in Vidyya*, April 2, 2003. http://216.86.213.73/today/v3i209_5.htm.

Glen Rangwala, "Claims and Evaluations of Iraq's Proscribed Weapons," Traprock Peace Center, March 18, 2003. http://trap rockpeace.org.

Reuters, "Firm Launches Kids' Masks for Bio-Warfare," Miscellaneous Anthrax Articles—Part I, April 3, 2002. http://anthrax investigation.com.

——, "Senate's Doctor Prescribes Biowar Safe Room," Miscellaneous Anthrax Articles—Part I, April 13, 2002. http://anthrax investigation.com.

Ken Ringle, "The Ancient History of a Bacterium: Anthrax Scares Go Way Back," *Washington Post*, October 27, 2001. www.washington post.com.

Barbara Hatch Rosenberg, "Anthrax Attacks Pushed Open an Ominous Door," Federation of American Scientists, September 22, 2002. www.fas.org.

George Rosie, "UK Planned to Wipe Out Germany with Anthrax: Allies World War Two Shame," SundayHerald.com, October 14, 2001. www.sundayherald.com.

David M. Sasaki, "Anthrax and Bioterrorism," Hawaii Department of Health, July/August 2003. www.state.hi.us.

Michael Schommer and Bill Hartmann, "State Veterinarian Urges Northwestern Minnesota Livestock Producers to Consider Anthrax Vaccinations for Their Grazing Cattle," Minnesota Board of Animal Health, June 26, 2002. www.bah.state.mn.us.

K. Scott, "Anthrax: Is Your Pet or Farm Dog at Risk?" *K9 Perspective,* 2003. www.k9magazinefree.com.

Jeff Shields, "Vets Trained to Spot Animal Symptoms of Biological/ Chemical Attacks," *Philadelphia Inquirer,* April 6, 2003. www. philly.com.

Mark Simkin, "Japan Unit 731," ABC (Australian Broadcasting Corporation) Online, April 22, 2003. www.abc.net.au.

Stephanie Simon, "For Cattlemen, Anthrax Just Another Aggravation," *Los Angeles Times,* October 29, 2001. www.latimes.com.

Thira Sirisanthana and Arthur E. Brown, "Anthrax of the Gastrointestinal Tract," *Emerging Infectious Diseases,* July 2002. www. cdc.gov.

Norman A. Suverly, Bill Kvasnicka, and Ron Torell, "Anthrax: A Guide for Livestock Producers," University of Nevada, Reno, Cooperative Extension, 2003. www.unce.unr.edu.

Morton N. Swartz, "Recognition and Management of Anthrax— an Update," *New England Journal of Medicine,* November 29, 2001. http://content.nejm.org.

David Thain, "State Veterinarian Reports Anthrax Outbreak," College of Agriculture, Biotechnology, and Natural Resources, University of Nevada, Reno, August 16, 2000. www.ag.unr.edu.

Kenneth Todar, "*Bacillus anthracis* and Anthrax," University of Wisconsin at Madison, Department of Bacteriology, 2001. www.bact. wisc.edu.

Peter C.B. Turnbull, "Anthrax Vaccines: Past, Present, and Future," *Vaccine,* 1991. www.anthrax.mil.

U.S. Department of Agriculture, "Anthrax," USDA Fact Sheet: "Anthrax,"October, 2001. www.usda.gov.

Vaccination News, "Anthrax Jab Rejected by Half Troops, *Vaccination Newsletter,* February 11, 2003. www.vaccinationnews.com.

Virgil, *The Georgics,* Internet Classics Archives. http://classics.mit. edu/Virgil/georgics.html.

G.F. Webb, "A Silent Bomb: The Risk of Anthrax as a Weapon of Mass Destruction," Stanford Graduate School of Business, March 17, 2003. http://faculty-gsb.stanford.edu.

Christopher L. Woolverton, Oleg D. Lavrentovich, and Gary D. Niehaus, "Virus Detected in Minutes Using Computer Display Technology," Kent State University Office of Technology Trans-

fer and Economic Development, May 26, 2002. www.techtrans.
kent.edu.

World Health Organization, "Guidelines for the Surveillance and
Control of Anthrax in Humans and Animals," WHO/EMC, 2003.
www.who.int.

Bob Worn, "U.S. Biological Experiments," Freedomwriter.com,
May 1, 2003. www.freedomwriter.com.

Websites

Alliance for Human Research Protection (www.researchprotection.
org). This website is dedicated to advancing responsible and eth-
ical medical research practices, such as anthrax vaccine studies.

Anthrax Vaccine Immunization Program (www.anthrax.osd.mil).
This official Department of Defense anthrax information website provides comprehensive information about human anthrax
and human anthrax vaccinations.

Department of Veterans Affairs (www.va.gov). This website contains information about topics of interest to veterans, including
Gulf War syndrome, insurance, compensation, appeals, and vo-
cational rehabilitation.

North Dakota State University College of Agriculture (www.
ag.ndsu.nodak.edu). This website contains extensive information about agriculture and animal husbandry, including anthrax,
natural resources, food, nutrition, and food safety.

Index

Picture Credits

Cover photo: © Dennis Kunkel/Phototake
© AFP/CORBIS, 20, 61, 62, 66, 69
AP/Wide World Photos, 57, 58, 76, 79, 82, 83
© Adrian Arbib/CORBIS, 22
© Bettmann/CORBIS, 31
Blackbirch Press Archives, 37
CDC/Public Health Image Library, 12 (both), 27
© CORBIS SYGMA, 43
© Corel Corporation, 25, 39
© Richard Ellis/CORBIS SYGMA, 49
Chris Jouan, 13, 14, 28, 71
Laguna Design/Photo Researchers, Inc., 72
© Michael S. Lewis/CORBIS, 40
Library of Congress, 52
© PhotoDisc, 17, 33
© The Pierpont Morgan Library/Art Resource, NY, 9
© Reuters NewMedia Inc./CORBIS, 55
© Sankei Shimbun/CORBIS SYGMA, 64–65
© Ariel Skelley/CORBIS, 46
© James A. Sugar/CORBIS, 75
© Dung Vo Trung/CORBIS SYGMA, 19

About the Author

Barbara Saffer, a former college instructor, has Ph.D. degrees in biology and geology. She grew up in New York City, has lived in Florida, Louisiana, Alabama, and Tennessee, and did research in many parts of the United States and Canada.

Barbara has written books about science, geography, exploration, famous people, and historical events, and her stories, articles, poems, and puzzles have appeared in numerous children's magazines. The author has also written fun mystery books for children, starring private detective Shannon Holmes and her parrot Lucky. Barbara's first book in the Diseases and Disorders series was *Smallpox*.

Barbara lives in Chattanooga, Tennessee, with her husband, two children, and pets.